African Initiations

African Initiations

Rites of Passage through the
Eyes of an Initiate

Shakmah Winddrum

Copyright © 2005 by Shakmah Winddrum.
Library of Congress Number: 2004099947
ISBN: 1-4134-6049-6

All rights reserved. No part of this book may be reproduced or transmitted in any form or by any means, electronic or mechanical, including photocopying, recording, or by any information storage and retrieval system, without permission in writing from the author.

This book was printed in the United States of America.

Contents

Acknowledgments 9
Introduction 11

Chapter 1
    Preface 15
    Pregnancy and Childbirth 17

Chapter 2
    Preface 26
    Scarification 27

Chapter 3
    Preface 40
    The Transition Ritual 42

Chapter 4
    Preface 50
    The Ritual Of Manhood and Womanhood 52

Chapter 5
    Preface 61
    The Rites of Independence 62

Chapter 6
    Preface 65
    The Secret Rites of Marriage 67

Chapter 7
    Preface 75
    Initiation Into Magick 77

Chapter 8
　Preface 88
　The Blood Rituals for Initiation 90

Chapter 9
　Preface 101
　The Death Rites of Passage 103

Chapter 10 110
　Preface 110
　Drumming 113

Final Thoughts 121
Suggested Exercises 123
Supplemental Reading 136

I dedicate this to my four gifts from heaven:

Mark Ivan Branche
Stanley Everett Branche Jr.
Wilma Branche-Ward
Alexander Gilbert Branche

Acknowledgments

An idea starts with one person, but by the time this idea comes to fruition, there have been many people responsible for it coming to life. I must confess this book, *African Initiations*, is a divine project which started many processes for me to be a better person. Those people who believed in this subject and who nurtured it through its development by way of inspiring me are to be hailed as warriors.

I give thanks to Joyce James for her typing, retyping, and more typing; to Lyratah who read, reread, and read some more; to Leticia Nixon who is a human Memorex and an unbelievable researcher. I give thanks to everyone who supported my dream, especially Ahbreem, who lovingly nagged me into madness; Ahvmeene and Hishamah, who massaged me into wellness; and my beloved Montorrah, the celestial chef who healed me through her wondrous cuisine; not to forget Mishanavah and Ahjudah, who just loved me for being.

Above all, my deepest gratitude to Dolores Ashcroft-Nowicki and Herbie and Jacks Brennan who believed this work was necessary for this time. Thanks, thanks, thanks!

We are all so blessed. Just take the time to look and say, "We give thanks."

Introduction

Little did I know then that one day this little girl named Anna from Chester, Pennsylvania, USA, would be so deeply involved with her African roots. First of all, I never wanted to be an African because they were always killed or captured in every Tarzan movie that I saw as a child. Second, these Africans lived in places that I couldn't even pronounce the names of, and third, as a child, I knew that everyone was afraid of Africans who wore strange-looking clothes, carried swords and spears, and lived in grass huts that were so small and looked most uncomfortable. But even worse than that, they jumped up and down and screamed at the top of their voices all around an open fire. No sir, I sure didn't want to be an African. And I was not the only one who believed as I did since the Hollywood moving pictures (as they were called then) were basically our source of knowledge. I remember once that someone wanted to send all of us Negroes back to Africa. I asked my teacher how I could go back to some place that I have never been. The answer was, "Sit down and be quiet!"

Once a year, we had Negro History Week to honor the likes of Frederick Douglass, Paul Lawrence Dunbar, Mary McLeod Bethune, Booker T. Washington, Sojourner Truth, and other "Negroes" who had helped their race. Very little was taught about Africa because so little had ever been written.

But somewhere really deep inside of me, the name Africa excited me. Secretly, I loved the way they looked, the way they danced, the way they sang. Even though, as a child, I was ashamed of Africans because they were always shown to be stupid and subservient. Actually, it seemed they were afraid of all white people, who took over their lives and country. I couldn't be proud of that, and I wasn't, even though as a child, deep in my heart, I longed for Africa.

Africa, oh, Africa, I need to understand you, I need to be with you, I think I love you—those were my thoughts for many years until I finally did return to Africa. I knew part of the truths. I knew part of the lies. But I knew that I was African, and I knew that I was proud and happy to finally be free to acknowledge and accept willingly my history, my heritage, and above all, my ancestors.

And I didn't have to reinvent myself; I just started to be African because I was never anything else all along. Thanks to the likes of Angela Davis, Stokely Carmichael, Martin Luther King Jr., Maya Angelou, Toni Morrison, and so, so many others who laid the groundwork for me to be my true self, armed with pride, courage, and purpose. This was the continuation of my African initiation and of my understanding of ancestral and deity worship that all Africans embrace.

Even though I have been raised as a Christian Methodist, there was plenty of space within me to relearn the ancient ways of my ancestors. My ancestors, who were slaves as a result of being shipped through Benin, Africa, to the southern portion of the United States, became the beginning for me. I quickly embraced the pure and simple way of giving thanks for my existence because of the courage, strength, perseverance, and the will to live that resulted in my being here today to talk about it.

I believe that ancestors, which is just another word for relatives who have died, are acknowledged in all societies somehow and somewhere. Perhaps this may not be in the body of a religion but within the accepted holidays, such as Veteran's Day or Memorial Day, when we in the United States celebrate our fallen warriors as well as those still alive. We are encouraged to display our flag and to place wreaths of flowers on our family graves. This is the same principle of the Africans who honor their ancestors. Then there is

November 1st, All Saints Day, set aside by Christians to pray for their deceased, which is observed November first, second, and third in many countries and is deeply religious. Asian traditions honor their dead every day using incense sticks, photographs, sweet cakes, and candies in the home as well as cemeteries.

Ancestor worship is not new or strange; it is respect. The African belief is that the ancestor has great influence with the deities that govern our lives as well as our destinies. Therefore, if we don't shower our departed ones with gifts of food, drink, song and dance, bad times lie in wait for us.

I have come face to face with my immortality knowing that I too will become an ancestor, eventually. It is quite comfortable knowing that I will never be forgotten.

Chapter 1

Preface

There is nothing that you can compare with the birth of a baby. I can remember the very first time that I saw a newborn baby girl named Serena, my first cousin. I was not impressed. I suppose being five years old had a lot to do with it. There was so much excitement with neighbors and family running in and out of the house, and nobody stopped to explain anything to me. When the doctor arrived, there was more frantic movement; I was pushed out of the room, and the door closed in my face. All I could think of was that this little wrinkly thing that looked like a bald mouse was taking my place and without my permission.

I have since learned that the birth of a child brings forth different responses and a myriad of emotions to everyone involved. It doesn't seem to matter how many children are in the family; the arrival of a new baby touches an emotion that is reserved just for that occasion. Oddly enough, after a few months, the new baby joins the ranks of all the other children and settles in to the routine of family life.

As a child, I never understood why a baby had to be christened, but I loved the occasion. It was a chance to be dressed in your Sunday best, a lot of people bringing all kinds of good food, plenty of laughter and mingling, and the oohs and aahs, with the "she looks like your mother" or whoever, or "what long fingers she has." Everyone carefully scrutinized the baby. The preacher arrived, and the ritual began. Years later, I would ask why we never took our babies to the church to be baptized. I never received an answer.

The baptism of a newborn is practiced in so many interesting and different ways that I decided to venture into other traditions that acknowledge childbirth and baptism in some manner. I found this aspect of the African traditions to be one that I could personally relate to what happened in my family at this special time.

Pregnancy and Childbirth

The arrival of a newborn in any tradition induces a euphoric atmosphere for the entire family, and many times the community, and sometimes, even the world.

With the announcement of the coming birth, arrangements begin immediately, and concerted attention is given to the expectant mother.

The ritual of the guessing game now starts. How does the mother-to-be look? How does she feel? When is she due? What did she eat? How often does she have morning sickness and is it the morning or is it at night? Is it more than one that she is carrying? Is her stomach pointed or rounded? Is the vein in her neck throbbing fast or slow? Through these signs, a boy or a girl can be determined by the old women of the village. These women have no scientific or medical backgrounds—they just know. To them, giving birth is not medical or scientific; it is of nature, and you learn everything about nature because nature teaches you everything you need to know in order to survive.

The phenomenon of birth on any level—animal, creature, or human—is highly respected, and it is celebrated through rituals of acknowledgment, praise, and gratitude. Yet there are some tribes that mourn the birth of a child and celebrate the death of a person.

This event of mourning is based on a belief that this new being has come into a world of trouble, pain, and misery, and tears should be shed for this innocent victim.

Once a pregnancy is announced, there are many dos and don'ts that move into action. These actions are not believed as old wives' tales or superstitions; rather they are fully accepted as instructions from the deities and must be obeyed to the fullest if a successful pregnancy is to take place. Every woman is constantly reminded that she must look at only beauty; she must never gaze at anything that is ugly, deformed, or frightening because she will "mark" her child and that ugliness will appear in her baby. On the other hand, if a woman craves certain foods, the shape of that food will appear as a birthmark somewhere on the child's body. If any animal, such as a snake or a lion, frightens an expectant mother, then that creature becomes the "totem" or animal guide for that child. Throughout the child's life, that animal becomes a lucky charm, a protector, a friend, and even a deity to worship and adore.

There are times when a baby is born with a deformity or a prominent "birthmark" that resembles an animal or bird. It is at this time that the infant is dedicated for life to that animal or bird. It is the responsibility of the village medicine man to confirm the name and characteristics of that deity.

A tribal belief that certain gods and goddesses would sire a child still holds fast today. A child born with strong characteristics, both physical and/or psychological, would be dedicated to that particular deity for life. For example, a child born unable to walk is recognized as a child of the snake or serpent deity. Or a child born blind is identified with the deity that administers justice. These deformities or afflictions can be an omen of ill will or a blessing for prosperity for the entire tribe, according to the status of the child's family.

There are cases of debilitating abnormalities at a child's birth that are classified as an evil omen or a curse on the mother and the entire family and, many times, even the entire village. It is then that certain measures are taken by the community to ward off this evil force or, as it is called, the anger of the gods.

It is a fact that Native American Indians would drown or leave a deformed infant to die because such a child would be a tremendous liability on the tribe and would never be able to survive the harsh and difficult life that had to be endured. It has been rumored that during World War II, the babies born to German mothers had to have blue eyes and Aryan features or they were left to starve to death. Many times, these babies would be used for gross experiments.

To assure that a baby would be protected and remain healthy throughout pregnancy, the expectant mother would bathe each day with herbs that the village elders or medicine man prepared. Palm oil or other essences would be used to massage the abdomen as it grows in size. In some tribes, once a woman confirms her pregnancy, she was no longer allowed to have sexual intercourse during her gestation period. It was believed that the infant would be jealous and angry with his father for disturbing him as well as taking the attention of his mother away from him. When the child would be born, there would be some antagonism between the child and the father because the child would never forget the disrespect the father had for him or her and its mother. If the baby was a girl and the father had sexual relations with the mother during the pregnancy, then it is believed that the girl child would be promiscuous all of her life.

In many tribes, men always have more than one wife for the reason of not being able to be with a pregnant wife, and if the second wife became pregnant, a third wife is added. By the time the third or even the fourth wife became pregnant, then the first wife would once again be available.

Since many tribal women had experienced circumcision, sexual intercourse was not exactly pleasurable or even missed. The circumcision of women will be discussed in detail later in the book.

When a woman begins her labor, the rites also begin. The birthing site is set up by the midwives of the village. There is a particular hut or forest area that has been cleared and is private. Palm leaves and a mixture of leaves that are prepared to ease the labor pains are spread out for the expectant mother to either stoop, kneel, or lie upon. At the time that these preparations are being performed, songs are being sung to encourage the baby to come quickly, to come unafraid, to come completely healthy, to come bringing good news from the gods, to come strong and wise. Once the water breaks (amniotic fluid flows), the moaning and groaning by the midwives intensifies. Strong herbal potions are given to the mother as well as the midwives who keep the chanting and moaning at a high pitch. Some tribes will bring the father into the hut or birthing place in order to bear witness of his child's birth. He too is given the potion to drink. At the moment of birth, the infant is placed on the mother's bare chest, and a few drops of the herbal potion are given to the baby.

Shrill screams from the midwives announce the arrival of the baby. Once the umbilical cord is cut, the "afterbirth" (placenta) is given to the father who decides where it is to be buried. The baby is cleaned with oil, as well as the mother, then both are allowed to rest. The chieftain of the tribe is officially notified; after which, the medicine man or "witch doctor" begins the preparations for the initiation rites.

According to the ancestral laws of each tribe, exact rituals must be performed within hours of birth and/or a certain number of days after the birth. For example, the entire village will celebrate with the family of the new infant. A circle, the "Ring of Presentation," is formed around the double set of grandparents who receive the newborn from the medicine man. The grandfathers pass the child back and forth three times and then return the infant to the medicine man who gives the baby to the grandmothers, and they pass the infant back and forth between them three times. The medicine man raises the child to the sky as he walks around the circle saying prayers and incantations. As he passes each person in the circle, a small gift is placed on the ground. The gift may be a feather, a small stone or rock, a bead or a necklace, a seed, or even an egg. When the child is returned to the maternal grandmother, the mother and father walk in opposite directions within the circle in order to gather the gifts and to give thanks to everyone.

It is at this time the marks of the deity are branded on the baby. Usually, the first scars are placed on the cheeks by the medicine man using a razor blade or a ritual knife. As soon as the cuts are bleeding, a poultice is applied to ensure the mark will be raised after healing. The father then parades with the screaming child around the circle, after which, another small gift is placed on the ground. The paternal grandparents walk in opposite directions to retrieve the gifts. The reasons why the grandparents walk the circle in different directions is to make sure that the bloodlines of the ancestors were properly mixed and not to insult either bloodline. Each bloodline would be considered as the first to circle and not the last to follow. This protocol was very important to acknowledge the status of the families. Everybody was important. Actually, the circling of the grandparents allowed them to show their pride in front of the entire village, as well as to be important participants and not just bystanders. This celebration included all of the family members from both the paternal and maternal sides of the family.

By this time, the mother has been given the baby to suckle. Meanwhile, the baby's naming will take place within three, six, or nine months. Once the character has been determined, the name will be given. Every name has a definite meaning with a story behind it. Some tribes require that part of the name represent the day or time of birth, or the deity, or some part should represent some facet of nature, or some part of the name should represent a deceased relative. However, in most tribes, a child is never named after a living person. When the Christian element entered the tribal culture, then Christian names were added to the list.

It should be noted that in many tribes, the mother is represented by one of the midwives because a woman cannot partake in any ritual while she is "bleeding" (menses).

The reason for separating women who are on the menses cycle varies from religion to religion. However, a shamanistic belief is that the woman is spending that "bleeding" time with the Great Mother. If she has menstrual cramps, the Great Mother is angry with her, or if her cycle lasts a long time, it is because the Great Mother wants to spend more time teaching her. There are some beliefs that a woman is not clean at that time of the month and should be separated from the "public." She is not allowed to cook or handle any food or cooking products. Yet there are others who believe that this "bleeding" is a sacred and honorable time for women, and the village honors these women.

Once the woman finishes the "birth bleeding," she must wait for three months before she has any sexual relations with her husband. Similar rules were being practiced as recently as thirty years ago in my family when women actually had to stay in bed for one month and then stay in the house for another month before she could go outside or receive visitors. This action was to allow time for the womb to move back into place, as well as for the rest of her body to properly heal. Oddly enough, this custom was practiced throughout my neighborhood. Later, I discovered that these "rules" were cultural. However, modern medicine began to dictate otherwise, and now, thirty years later, the custom has died out completely in the Western world and is influencing Africa in the same way.

It was also at this time that she "knitted" with her baby and could observe closely the characteristics that were necessary for the future naming of the child.

If the child were born dead, the midwives would loudly grieve instead of making the shrill scream of celebration. The baby's body would be washed quickly in water, and then oil would be applied, after which, the body would be wrapped in leaves and taken away to be buried in the forest in a secret space. The afterbirth (placenta) would also be buried with it. After three days of mourning, the woman was expected to resume her usual life until she became pregnant again. However, her husband still had to wait the prescribed three months in order for her to heal. It was not unusual for the woman to avoid her husband strongly and adamantly for even a longer period of time. Sometimes, the medicine woman had to resew the opening to the vagina, which is painful enough without the act of intercourse before a certain amount of healing. Also, she is not too happy to have to go through being a virgin again. She is angry, upset, frightened, and there is not too much she can do about it except to ask her husband to wait for her to heal. The husband usually accommodates his wife.

If the woman dies because of childbirth and the baby lives, then the husband's second wife takes charge of the infant. If there is no second wife yet, then the maternal grandparents take care of the child until the husband remarries.

If both mother and child die, they are buried immediately together; the belief being that the baby decided not to come to earth at this time but didn't want to be separated from his mother, and she decided to go back with him. Still, a ritual of celebration is held by the village for the mother and child to have a good journey and to send blessings back to the village.

Godparents, as the Western world knows them, perform a different function within the villages. In fact, the term "godparent" is not used; however, it is used now to illustrate the duties and responsibilities of the "second" parents. The second parents are chosen by the deities to oversee the rearing of the child if anything happens to the birth parents or if the grandparents are deceased. If the father is away from the village for a long period of time for any reason, then the godparent takes on the responsibility of guiding that child in the ways of the ancestors. To be a representative of the deities in a child's life, is a highly honored and privileged position, and it is not usually taken lightly

Once the ritual of the Ring of Presentation is completed, the medicine man and the male elders of the village join the father and the newborn in the medicine hut in order to receive the infant's secret name. Cowry shells, polished stones, or snake bones are thrown upon the ground by the medicine man. The medicine man is somewhat equivalent to a minister of the church. However, his duties reach out much further than preaching and teaching. The medicine man in an African village is considered as a messenger to the deities and the ancestors. He also has been gifted with special magical powers that can be used to heal, to destroy, or to control the elements, such as rain and fire. He also serves as judge and jury in so much as he is capable of making decisions on every aspect of village life. He is highly respected and deeply feared by everyone because of his magical powers. The influence of the medicine man is accepted because he is able to cause success or failure in the village. The tradition of the medicine man exists today because the villagers never stopped believing in the power and knowledge of this position.

Then each elder, having been properly initiated throughout his life, is allowed to "receive through spirit" the interpretation of the bones, shells, or stones. His father or mother must never speak the infant's name aloud or even in public.

Once the name has been decided upon, the father returns the infant to the mother. After being told her baby's secret name, she then gives a nickname or an acceptable name that the public may use. During the child's life, his secret name will be used only in specific rituals, and even then, his name will be spoken only in undertones out of anyone's hearing range. There are different traditions in naming a child; however, every child has a secret name given to him or her by the deities they worship. For fear of having evil curses put on them, no birth data or secret name is ever revealed. There is a strong belief that if anyone knows the day and exact time that a child was born, many evil spirits would be able to control and dictate to the child forever. The secret name is to identify the child to the ancestors and deities that will protect him for his entire life. Therefore, spiritual names, such as the names of animals, rivers, or flowers, were given for public use. This practice is very important for the villagers and certainly sacred, even though it might be difficult for others to really understand the true significance of the whole ritual.

The child's birthday is the day of his official naming ceremony. The naming ceremony could be within three, six, nine, or twelve months after the child's birth. The village elders decide the exact time as well as the type of ritual to be conducted. This day is recorded on all government records and school records.

In preparation for the ritual, the father is expected to walk alone in the forest or jungle and kill the first snake he finds. He brings the snake to the medicine man who "reads" the dead snake as an oracle. Every part of the snake will be used by the medicine man in his healing practice. The bones of the snake will be used to make up a pouch or a charm for protection, good health, and good fortune. Another talisman is made for good harvest, good health, and protection and given to the father. The mother is given a small talisman from the snake's body to enhance her fertility.

Once the medicinal and religious operation on the snake has been completed, the meat is cooked and served to the villagers, unless it was an extremely venomous snake. In that case, it is burned to ashes which are then used by the medicine man in his medicinal formulas.

The extremely high value placed on a woman's ability to be fertile exists in the modern world as much as it existed in the beginning. A middle eastern king was forced to divorce his beloved queen because of her inability to conceive. Science, as well as shamanistic technologies, could not bring the desired birth to this loving couple, and he, the king, was forced by tradition to marry a younger woman who could and did birth heirs to the throne.

The African man's strong desire to have his bloodline continue throughout time is one of the reasons he would acquire more wives. It would seem that the more children a man would sire, the higher his status would be in the village.

Of course, having many wives was, and still is, a common and accepted practice in many parts of the world. Making a religious act of having no more than five wives means no one can dispute the religious law. However, women cannot have five husbands. Although this practice has been banned by modern society in certain parts of the world, the practice continues in other parts of the world.

Chapter 2

Preface

I was always called a scaredy-cat as a child because I could not tolerate any kind of pain. When all of my little girl friends had their ears pierced, they were considered to be cute and precious. I opted not to be cute and precious if it meant sticking a needle into my earlobe. It was bad enough to have to wear shoes that always hurt my feet, but I thought everybody's feet hurt in shoes. I cried when I saw a horse having shoes nailed into its hoofs. If the horse didn't feel the pain, I surely did. When I first saw a tattoo on a man, I thought he used a stencil to paint it on his chest and arms. Never in my wildest thoughts would I ever have believed that this was the work of a needle piercing the skin. I would have fainted. Just thinking about the plucking of eyebrows pains me.

I was so curious as to why people subjected themselves to the agony of mutilating their bodies. Why, for goodness' sake, why? I soon learned the reasons why this so-called mutilation was important to so many people from all kinds of traditions. This act of piercing and painting the body goes back a long way, with meanings that I still don't understand. So, here is what I discovered for my own understanding and acceptance.

Scarification

Body decoration is not a new phenomenon, nor is it a symbol of barbarism. There are as many reasons for decorating the body as there are people who do it, whether it would be for the gods or the latest fashion or style. Body decoration makes a powerful statement in defining who you are and how you want to be acknowledged by your gods or your peers.

Men, women, and children experience some form of body decoration or scarring at least once in their lifetime, whether that be ear piercing, tattooing, shaving of hair from various parts of the body, eye make-up, fingernail and toenail cutting and painting.

The modern-day world of scarification is accepted without question or distaste in the form of breast implants, tummy tucks, liposuction, and other body modification. All of this is to make a statement of who you are. This is the same premise for tribal scarification, no more distasteful but for different purposes.

Scarification has always been used to identify the tribe as well as to identify the deity or god or goddess to whom the individual has been dedicated. Some scarring may take place immediately after birth; many villages conduct the first marking rituals between three and six months of age.

The medicine man of the village begins the preparation of the ritual by gathering herbs to make ointments, salves, and drinks. The medicine man is the only person allowed to "operate" since he is the most powerful man or woman in the village. He meets with the elders in order to determine the worthiness of the child and the family. Once the oracles have been read and the divine message has been understood and agreed upon, the ceremony will begin.

If the child is a boy, his ritual begins at dawn with the rising of the sun. If the child is a girl, her ritual begins at midnight during the full moon.

There is always a circle formed by the villagers surrounding a huge fire in the center. This formation represents mankind surrounding the gods and goddesses. The elders and the medicine man sit in the east so that the first rays of the sun (or moon) fall on them so that they have the new power of the day. Usually, there are more than just a couple of babies being prepared for this ritual, so the excitement and high energy fuel the drumming and singing to invoke the deities. The naked babies are screaming their loudest, unaware of what is about to come.

Each child's family has been told by the medicine man to bring a black chicken (for a girl) or white chicken (for a boy) for sacrifice to the deity. In addition to the chicken, a ruling deity may also request another animal (lamb, piglet, pigeons, wild boar, or monkey) which the family is also obliged to provide for sacrifice.

Animal sacrifice has been practiced since biblical times with very few explanations given. The African believes that animals represent the characteristics of the deities. They believe that the animals are the messengers of the gods. To sacrifice them is to honor them, and to eat them after the completion of the sacrificial ritual is to gain their strength and wisdom. Each animal represents a particular god or deity. Signifying the greatness of the god will demand a great animal. The male gods usually demand a bull or a ram to be sacrificed. The blood of the bull is given to everyone to drink and to smear on the body in order to absorb and receive the strength of the animal. It is also believed that animals are cunning, strong, and brave, as well as keen on surviving, as man must be. Therefore, men work hand in hand with nature by understanding the animals' characteristics and motives and by understanding the value of every creature's existence.

The sacrificial animals are venerated by being bathed, decorated with feathers and leaves, honored with song, and bestowed with gratitude for their role in the sacrifice. To each, the medicine man explains the reasons for its sacrifice as if the animal understands the need for its death. One reason given to the animal may be that the deity has requested its death by way of the dreams of the medicine man or possibly because the elders want more protection from warring tribes or even to stop plagues or a drought.

The first cut in the ceremony is to the sacrificial animals, whose blood is quickly collected by the mother. The father then smears the collected blood over the entire body of the child under the watchful eyes of the elders and medicine man. Once the baby is covered with the animal's blood, his father and mother raise it to the heavens in all directions in order to receive the blessings from the universe. The baby is then washed with herbs and water. The sacrificed animal is removed to be cleaned for cooking and later to be eaten.

The medicine man takes a huge drink of an herbal potion made to enhance and deepen his spirit connection and communication but does not swallow; instead, he sprays the baby in four areas. First, each side of the cheeks, each side of the upper arms, each side of the chest, and then each side of the upper back. Before the child has time to finish reacting to this spraying, a cut is made into the child's flesh. The baby's body is cut in four places representing the four corners of the universe. (Interestingly enough, the concept of the four quarters of the universe is represented on all levels of the African belief systems. In the minds of the villagers, air, water, fire, and earth are known as sky gods, being air elements; the animal gods being fire elements; man gods being the water elements, and the earth gods being the ancestors, represent the earth elements.) These cuts may symbolize wards for protection from evil spirits, abundant harvest, protection from warring tribes, strong fertility, and/or being an honest and good member of the tribe. Sometimes, a design must be made according to the desires of the deity or they may be simple straight lines. Whatever the case may be, the cuts are completed rapidly.

Immediately, the medicine man applies a black sticky poultice containing antibiotic properties to the bleeding wounds in order to ensure proper healing and scarification. The poultice is applied to the cuts after each daily bath until they begin to heal in one to two weeks. Dark skin may form a keloid naturally, but the poultice ensures the scars will be raised and not become infected. The scars are then there for life

With the screams of the sacrificed animal, the screams of the infant, and the screams of the villagers, the celebratory frenzy increases. Each baby is blessed and anointed one at a time in front of the elders and the medicine man. For each child, the medicine man takes a drink of his potion. As the ceremony progresses, the medicine man may start to dance or sing, or he may sit or stand as the invoked deities arrive "on his head."

Having a deity "on his head" is a form of possession by spirit—a trancelike condition that resembles the physical and spiritual attributes of the particular deity that has been invoked. It is believed that the deity enters the host through the back of the head, taking complete control of the entire body. The deity may hop around on one leg, walk bent over, or even just sit to listen to the petitioners. Deities have been known to demonstrate their strength and bravery by thrusting swords or knives into the stomach of the possessed, drinking full bottles of alcohol in one swallow, and even dancing on hot coals. These deities "show off" by performing dangerous feats in order to demand respect and instill fear. Whatever the deity wants, the deity gets; he is a god to be obeyed, honored, and worshipped. When the deity exits from the back of the head of the host, he or she is exhausted and confused and must rest for some time. Even so, another deity may decide to come into the picture, and the host must oblige with full participation according to what the deity demands.

The participants know every deity according to the type of speech, which could be abusive or kind: or the actions which could be wild and unruly or gentle and compassionate. All of the villagers know exactly what to do and what to prepare for each deity that "appears." Some deities require certain foods that are prepared in a prescribed manner. They could be excessively cooked with hot peppers or very salty or very sweet or void of animal meat—the list may go on and on. The deity may require the hosts to wear specific animal skins and certain bird feathers of a particular color, or even symbols painted on the face, chest, and arms. Each deity has its own peculiarity for its recognition to the villagers. Preciseness and exactness are necessary to satisfy the deity or he will become angry and cause mayhem and disaster to the village. Belief in the power and magic of the deity causes the medicine man to instruct the villagers in their responsibility. They must perform the proper behavior for each deity to avoid the anger and abandonment of that deity.

Meantime, the screaming baby is given an herbal type of tea to drink that soothes and quiets him enough to nurse from the mother. He is soon asleep from exhaustion. Meanwhile, the ritual is in full swing as prayers of praise and thanks are drummed, danced, and sung. Food is then served to the elders and the medicine man who, afterwards, retires as the villagers continue the celebration with feasting and dancing.

Other reasons for scarification vary with each tribe and village. In one instance, the lower lip is cut in order to encase a flat disc made of lightweight wood. This practice is started at an early age, and as the lip stretches, then larger discs are applied during ritual. The earlobes are also included in this method of scarification. The larger the disc, the more beautiful the person, since both men and women participate in this type of scarification. At one time, the belief for ear and lip stretching was to discourage warring tribes from kidnapping and raping their women. Slavers were disgusted at the sight because profits were not to be made with these abnormalities. On the other hand, the villagers were quite proud of their beauty.

Scarification by fire is a most important ritual that is performed throughout a villager's life in order to make him or her strong and brave. As with most initiation rites, the entire village must participate forming the Great Ring or the straight line. Definite choreography and rhythm is determined by the intent of the initiation. It is never pure abandonment and wild frenzy as has been portrayed dishonestly by the Western world. Indeed, every step, every movement, every gesture has a significant meaning and result. These songs, chants, mantras, and drum rhythms have been passed from generation to generation. Initiation is a sacred form of worship and is never forgotten or misunderstood.

I must digress for a moment here to address the importance of movement and sound in African ritual.

Such ritual movement as the Yanvolou is a good example of

invoking the deities as well as saluting and greeting them. This movement, which is a crouched position of the body with both hands placed on both knees, is likened to a serpentine action of the spine, shoulders, and head. The hips undulate to the slow steady pace of the drums. Every woman, man, and child takes part in this dance. It is truly infectious and great fun. The lower you crouch while doing this rolling-spine movement, the more you are applauded. Of course, the children excel, but then, quite a few adults are successful. What really matters is the proper salute and attitude to the deity.

One of the most uplifting and most spectacular ritual movements I have ever experienced is called the Mandala. There are hundreds of people forming a huge circle around the altar or fire and the elders. The movement is quite simple and easy to learn immediately. Two short side steps to the right, and two short side steps to the left. That's it. The beauty of this movement is the continuation of the steps by hundreds. A person can drop out at any time to rest and then join the circle later, but the movement must not be stopped until the elders call for the end. The energy is electrifying as the circle enlarges with more people joining in. The singing of songs over and over again with the two-step movement is truly a Mandala that transcends your spirit into realms that you never knew existed. It definitely has a hypnotizing effect on the consciousness. This Mandala has been performed for at least three days without stopping. Once the elders call everything to a gentle halt, you can believe, no one is ever the same again.

The songs that are sung usually tell stories about the deities; the characteristics, the promises, the petitions, the prayers, or the thank-yous. These songs are learned from childhood and will never be forgotten even if not understood. Sometimes the names of the deities are spoken aloud over and over again for hours. This is believed to cause the deity to be so tired of hearing his or her name called continually that they quickly arrive to the ritual. The deities will then do anything to shut up the voices. This repetitive song is labeled a mantra and is used by many traditions in one form or another. The primary reason for using a mantra in ritual is to cause the participant to focus on one point—spirit, deity, god, or goddess—while the body forgets about any discomfort.

Chants are basically the same as mantras, with the exception of the length of time they continue, and a monotone is used. Chants are closer to singing songs and have a distinct purpose of greeting the deity. The chant honors and salutes the deity. The mantra calls the deity into the ritual.

Gestures in rituals also salute and greet ancestral spirits and gods. For example, whenever a participating deity is mentioned in a song, the celebrant will quickly raise the right hand straight overhead and then tap the earth three times and continue singing. Sometimes the gesture may be tapping the heart area three times whenever an ancestor or deity is mentioned.

These gestures signify the intention of the participant to invite the deity into their hearts or to invite the deity to come down from the sky to the earth.

Another cutting for the baby is the hair off the head. If the baby is bald, the shaving is still done. In the past, before razor blades were introduced to the villages, razor-sharp stones were used to shave the head, but now, with technology reaching every part of the globe, it is not uncommon to hear and see automatic shavers. Yet there are some villages that prefer and maintain the old-fashioned way of cutting the first hair. Because of the experience of the medicine man, cutting the hair with the stone is not necessarily as painful as it is annoying. He knows how to move swiftly and accurately; besides, he is under the influence of the powerful deities he serves.

The cut hair or shavings are placed in a gourd that also contains a small amount of blood from the sacrificed animal along with its feathers, tongue, parts of the scrotum and tail (whichever may apply). These ingredients will be used to make a fetish medicine bag for the child's protection and good health.

Initiation is not an option; it is a duty, an obligation, and a responsibility. Every child grows up knowing well in advance that he or she must "go between the worlds" at different times of his or her life. There is much excitement, anxiety, and sometimes fear experienced by the initiates, but that is to be expected. When the rites of initiation were highly secret, the village would have an idea of what was going on but respected the rules of the elders not to inquire or pry. If such an invasion of a secret initiation should happen, then the perpetrator would be put to death or blinded along with the removal of the tongue so the individual could never reveal what he saw. This rarely happened because from an early age, one learns certain behaviors are not accepted.

Disciplining a child's behavior is the foremost priority in village life. A child cannot refuse a request or a command. There is never a response of no or I don't want to. There are no choices if a parent or elder decrees anything. The question is, why would the women subject their daughters or other youngsters to go through these tortuous experiences that will scar their minds forever? The answer is basically very simple: it is tradition, it is the ancestors, it is the will of the deities. Tradition dies hard in every religion or culture. Again, fear of fierce anger and punishment from the ancestors and deities for disobeying, fear of being ostracized by the village, fear of the elders who had the authority to seize everything you possessed and owned. Everyone surrendered to tradition until outside influences began to crack into these beliefs and these rituals; influences such as religious missionaries and humanitarian groups from other countries offering aid for better living. But the biggest factor for breaking tradition was the influence of learning how to read. A brand-new world was now opened to the villagers. The taste of a different world soon became more powerful than simple village life. The elders believed that they could handle both worlds. As a result, the Western world was welcomed into the physical Africa, but not the spiritual Africa. And in the beginning, the Western world wanted only the physical wealth of Africa and was grateful for the tradition of religions that kept the villagers occupied. We already know the rest of that story.

No one may touch an initiate's scars except the medicine man who may also be the ruler of that village. He, the medicine man, applies the oils and ointment to the scars, to observe their healing. The initiate cannot scratch himself with his hands; instead, he must use a twig or stick from a sacred tree. If the scars begin to heal badly, then evil spirits were attempting to enter into the body of the initiate. The ritual must be performed again, but this time in secret, with only the village elders and medicine man present. There is a great expense to the family for this secret ritual, but it must be done. Under the cloak of darkness, the group journeys quite a distance into the forest or jungle to be near a great river or river falls. This particular river initiation is for boys or men only; women have a different trek if they must go through another ritual of re-initiation.

This ritual is awesome, spectacular, and frightening, and it has been said that there have been some that did not survive the ritual—it was the will of the gods.

The females that must be re-initiated begin their ordeal by having to run through the forest carrying hot burning charcoal with their arms while being beaten with long thin branches taken from a sacred tree within or near the village compound. The elder women handle the whips and fire, as well as lead the girls to a sacred part of the river or a sacred cave. All the while this is going on, the girls are not to scream out in pain. The lead elder is beating a drum or bell to warn anyone who may be approaching to go in the opposite direction. This warning allows the intruder time to hide quickly in the forest—the consequences of seeing a secret ritual is known and understood by all.

Once the sacred place is reached, everyone collapses from exhaustion, but there is still much work to be done. Herbs and ointments are applied to the arms that have been seared. If it is a sacred cave, the initiate must squat in front of the cave, but her back is to the cave entrance. The same posture is assumed at the riverbanks. Since the fire run was started at dawn, the squatting must be held until the moon is visible to the elder women. There is no eating or drinking by anyone during the entire process. Fear of the departing demons who may enter the food and drink is a strong enough reason to honor this edict.

Invocation of the ancestors starts this phase of the process. Words of praise and honor and also giving thanks are said loudly by the women elders. This liturgy lasts about one hour and a half. When this is completed, the girls are excused to relieve themselves. Coming back to the assumed squat position, the invocation of the gods and goddesses by the elders continues for another two hours, making promises of gifts and deeds on behalf of the initiates. Once the moon has been sighted, the initiates rise and face the moon, and their song for forgiveness and praise begins. If a deity has been omitted, the initiate is beaten with the branches and must begin again. The women elders use their full strength with the whippings because they don't want to be out in the forest anyway and especially at night with no warriors to protect them. It is quite unusual for the initiates to make such a gross error.

The initiate is so worn out physically and emotionally that she really doesn't care about what is to happen next. The elders offer libations carefully made with a strong herbal potion to the demon guardians of the cave. Food from the girl's family, such as wheat cakes and rice, together with shells and precious stones, are handed to each girl who then places them on top of the poured libations. The elders remove her garments, and the initiate faces the opening of the dark cave. Detailed instructions are recited again and again by the lead elder, along with grave warnings and consequences. Silence must be maintained at all times as they prepare to meet the ancestors. The girls are reminded that one day, they too will be ancestors, so they remember this day with kindness and compassion. The fear was not relieved. Each girl walks into the dark opening at intervals, daring not to make even a whimper. Even the cave bats are already out on their nightly tasks; there are sounds of fluttering and flying, scurrying and crawling. And many times, critters and creatures move over the initiate's feet as they run for cover. The strong smells of old decay in the cave are putrid and stale. When all of the girls reach the stone altars, they prostrate themselves while the elders chant special prayers and ancient incantations. With arms stretched over their heads, the initiates roll to the right and then to the left, keeping their faces to the gritty, grimy ground. This action of humility and surrender is repeated seven times. Remember, if the girl is on her monthly menses, she is not allowed to participate in this ritual.

When the "dusting" is completed, the elder women enter the cave, chanting softly with prayers of forgiveness. A gourd prepared ahead of time with rain, river, or well water mixed with herbs and various leaves and bush roots is held high above the initiate's head. Slowly, the mixture is poured over the entire body of the initiate. No hands are permitted to touch any part of the body, only the herbal mixture. The types of herbs used have such strange and difficult names that it takes an expert of the region where it grows to know exactly what it is and what it does. This knowledge is passed from generation to generation and can only be found in that particular region. Each area produces different herbs, which are named with the language of the tribe. Even though a particular herb has a different name in each tribe, the use and the results may well be the same. Each village knows exactly what herb to use for their purposes of cleansing, healing, and/or cooking.

Again, the initiates assume the prostrate position and "dust" themselves after the elders leave the cave. This time, as they re-enter the cave, the elders sing softly to honor the deities. This time, the gourds are filled with a strong alcoholic brew that will bring on the same results as whiskey or beer. The homemade brew is poured over the heads of the girls as before so that the ancient deities feel honored and respected. The initiates dust themselves once more after the elders exit the cave.

When the elder women re-enter the cave for the third time, the singing ceases. In place of the singing come harsh words, abusive language, and admonitions to any evil that still remains and, again, the beating of the initiates with the long slim reeds. The lead elder woman raises her arm to stop all beating. From her pouch, she removes three small stones and places them in each of the initiate's mouths. The girls stand and remain standing and shivering and absolutely quiet. A small fire is started in order to shed some light in the cave for the work that has to be done. The head elder holds a "lightning stone" over the fire. No one is quite sure as to the origin of these medium-sized, smooth, oval, black stones, but the belief is that they are directly from the gods and hold immense power of magic. You must be a "high initiate" to use this tool of the gods. One end of the stone is heated until it begins to glow and sparkle. A slow melodic song is started by the elders, hardly above a whisper. The elder rises with the red, glowing end of the stone and proceeds to make new scars on each girl. The stones in the mouth prevent them from screaming aloud. First, the face on each side, both arms, and then the back of the shoulders. The assisting elders immediately apply the black poultice on the open bleeding wounds. Bleeding stops immediately, and the "lightning stone" is returned to the fire and watched over by one of the assistant elders; she then removes the glowing stone with sticks to the edge of the fire.

The initiates are given three gulps of a bitter drink that serves to lessen the pain and fear. Each girl is then instructed to remove one of the many skulls that fill the altar. She has to choose the one that calls her secret name; woe be unto her if she chooses the wrong skull. She must extend herself beyond the pain in order to hear the calling of her name—she must stand there until there is no question or doubt. The elder women stand behind them to prevent them from making a fatal error. They must have completed their choice before the fire dies out completely.

The initiate points to the skull of her choice; the lead elder agrees and gently lifts the skull from the altar, careful not to disturb any of the hundreds that are crowding the altar. The elder places the skull at the feet of the altar and then continues until each girl has made the correct choice. Just as the last embers of the fire start to fade, each girl is gently laid on her back with her head resting on the skull.

If a spider, a roach, or even a snake crawls or scurries out of the skull, it is believed that the ancestor and the god or goddess has ordained and blessed this re-initiation. The drug has started to take its effect on the girls in the form of release from pain through psychedelic experiences. The elder women quickly remove the stones from the relaxed mouths and then cover each girl with cloth or fabric provided by her family. The elders retreat to the outside of the cave to await the dawn.

Just before the first rays, the elders enter the cave clapping their hands rapidly. They assist the girls to their feet and place the cloth or fabric over their heads, covering their bodies entirely. The head elder carefully replaces each skull, kissing it three times. The girls are instructed to turn to face the altar. Everyone starts to slowly walk backwards, the elder women guiding the girls to the outside. Walking backwards is a gesture of respect and obeisance. One never shows one's backside to the deity. To turn your back to the altar is to disregard their presence and their status. Usually, as they walk backwards, they also bow their heads as a form of saluting and acknowledging that they are less than the deity. The stepping backward is slow and quiet, almost bowing and not having the right to look the deity in the eye. Once outside, they move the covered girls away from the opening as the bats start to appear.

A drink of water, wheat cakes, and some berries is given to everyone. The girls eat and drink from under their shrouds. Everyone then sits quietly while toilet breaks are taken. When all have returned to the circle, the lead elder hands each girl the branch or reed that was used to beat her. The initiate proceeds to break or tear apart the whip of her initiation, signifying the end of her ordeal. The walk back to the village is filled with singing, drum beating, or bell ringing in order to announce their arrival back to the compound. Everyone joins in with the singing, and the family of each girl comes forth to claim her, recognizing their cloth or fabric. The initiate must remain covered until she is inside of her family's home. She cannot be seen by anyone other than the elders and her family for seven days. She is allowed to sleep as much as she likes. When she does awaken, she eats and has her new scars attended to by the elder women who visit at least twice a day for that period of confinement. Of course, everyone is relieved that this particular initiation ritual is finished, especially the girl and her family.

Scarification is never taken lightly or disrespected in any way. It is a sacred tradition that has intense meaning to its participants. It is honored and understood for far more than any aesthetic value. Scarring is symbolic of the ancestral heritage being maintained throughout time. Each tribe has its particular and definite markings according to the will of the ancestors, as well as the gods and goddesses.

Today's scarification of ear piercing, seven or more on each ear, eyebrow piercing, tongue piercing, lip piercing, nipple piercing, navel piercing, genital piercing—all have their roots from these beloved and pure traditions. Body tattooing has always been a sacred and symbolic union with the gods and goddesses of all indigenous peoples. There are rites, rituals, and ceremonies conducted even today that we will never begin to understand or be allowed to witness because they are so sacred.

The fact remains that man has the driving need to "mark," in some fashion, his growth and development within the realms of god, spirit, and community. These "badges" of honor display courage, bravery, illumination, advancement, completion, achievement, and success. Whether you wear these "badges" on a uniform, a hat, or your skin, the significance is quite clear. You can be sure that each of these "badges" was awarded with pomp and circumstance, ceremonies, both public and private. The receiver stands at attention, silent, saluting at the completion, bowing in thanks, or just celebrating with friends who have like minds or like scars.

Chapter 3

Preface

I couldn't wait until I turned twenty-one years old. That was the magic age I heard about all of my life. I would be able to do anything I wanted, go anywhere I wanted, wear anything I wanted. I would be free! Free from "do this," "do that," "don't do that," "don't do this," "be home by 11:00 sharp," "no you can't." Oh, please hurry up, twenty-one years, please hurry fast. I was only six years old!

There was always something special that happened on holidays, birthdays, the beginning of winter, and even the beginning of spring within my family and neighborhood. To mark certain occasions, be it marriage, death, graduation, or engagement, was expected, no matter where you lived or how much money your family had. We would celebrate at the drop of a hat. It didn't take much to have a feast, a party, or a general get-together.

I was so caught up in the good times that we had on these party days; I asked if I could have a party to celebrate my first time to menstruate. Can you possibly imagine the dumbstruck look on my mother's and aunt's faces when I, with a great smile, asked that question? When they did speak, it was, "What institution should she be committed to?" as well as, "She has surely lost her mind. I've heard of women going crazy when they first get their period." Then came the fastest and hardest slap across the face and the side of my head with a, "Stop being fresh." I crept away and cried and cried.

After learning what other young boys and girls had to go through on "such occasions," I didn't feel so bad or ashamed or fearful. I soon found out how my brothers were circumcised; I almost fainted. Was this going to happen to me? I dared not ask because I knew I would be shipped out to some institution for sure. As the years passed, I prayed every night for two things: one was not to be cut open like my brothers, and two, that I could survive to be twenty-one. I did.

But there were many boys and girls who did not survive these "special occasions."

The Transition Ritual

A rite of passage is a celebration for everyone anywhere. The acknowledgment that one stage of life ends and another begins is understood worldwide and is practiced in one form or fashion by every organized religious group, as well as those who practice their individual beliefs.

Bar Mitzvah in the Jewish tradition, confirmation in the Roman Catholic tradition, the Native American's young warrior, or the African's young hunter, are all an accepted process of recognizing that adult responsibilities are close at hand. This is a very special time for the adolescent to take heed of the life that is awaiting them. As such, there are "tests" to be passed to indicate the readiness of the young candidate.

African rites of passage are used to determine the character and ability of the child. Who will be the hunter, the farmer, the healer, the scholar, the businessman, or the owner of a great herd is the question on the minds of the parents. Because the compound is basically small, the child is observed for certain characteristics long before the age for the rites of passage.

Seven-year-old boys are awakened just before dawn by their fathers and escorted to a remote area outside of the village compound.

After collecting the necessary gear, the group moves quietly out of the village. There is always an air of excitement and great anticipation for this auspicious occasion. Even though some of the young boys are seven years old, they have been preparing for this special event for at least three or four years, and they realize the importance of this turning point in their lives. Through informal training and play-acting, they learn how to make bow and arrows, spears, basic drum making, and of course, sling making. It is true that the training is informal and playful, but the ancient ways are also being preserved and passed on to another generation. These young boys will never forget this spectacular experience. It seems that they start the instruction as babies but return as young men. Tradition dictates every aspect of this initiation; nothing must be forgotten or deliberately left out by the fathers or their sons. Because this is not regarded as a secret ceremony, the entire community has participated in the preparations necessary for this transitional custom.

Regardless of the young boy's decision on his life's vocation, he is bound by custom to experience this level of initiation. In some ways, it is a sad period of time for the mothers who understand that their baby boy will "bite off the birth cord" in order to become a full-grown man, quite capable of fending for himself. There was also fear because of the unknown details of the ritual; all in all, it was the knowledge that you left as a child, but you would return as a man.

When the group arrived at the sacred grounds, the fathers begin to paint the son's bodies with designs that would be pleasing to the deities. Rhythmic chants and drumming begin as the intricate designs unfold over the entire body of the naked boy. Upon completion of the drawings, the medicine man and the elders form a straight line while hopping from one foot to another in sync with the drumbeat and chanting. The young boys form a straight line facing their fathers who, by this time, have joined the medicine man and the elders.

Strong drink is given to the boys who then start to dance and howl in a frenzy. Once the drink takes effect, one boy is taken from the group to a hidden place in the jungle. The father instructs the son to lie flat on his back with his legs spread. Each of the boy's arms and legs are held by one of the elders while the medicine man kneels between the boy's legs. Sprinkling a solution on the boy's genitals, the medicine man continues to chant and invoke the deities. The medicine man takes hold of the penis. If the young boy has an erection, it will make the cutting easier. If not, then the medicine man will massage the penis into an erection in order to complete the task. Holding the boy's penis in his hand, he quickly cuts off the foreskin. The blood rushes out from the wound; the boy's scream is heard by everyone. Poultice is applied, and a sacred tree leaf is used to bandage the entire penis. He is taken away by his father to make room for the next boy. The strong drink is again administered as the young boy writhes in agony.

The father escorts the limping tormented boy to a hut that has been constructed just for this purpose of circumcision. The boy is left in the hut alone until the other boys join him one by one. They do not speak or even look at one another. The only relief they have is knowing that the worst part is over. However, yet another agony that awaits them is the need to urinate.

Later on, the leaves are changed for more poultice and fresh leaves. The used leaves are burned in the center fire along with the foreskin from the cutting. While the boys are in the healing hut, a few of the men go out to hunt small game for the group's meal.

The medicine man decides that the ritual was a success and proceeds to lead a line dance with the fathers in order to give thanks to the ancestors and the deities. The fathers and medicine man will care for the boys for seven days; after which, they will return to the village compound amidst a joyous revelry for their manhood. Care for the wound still goes on under the watchful eye of the father and the medicine man. Healing does not take too long, perhaps four to six weeks. Part two of his initiation is soon to follow.

On the first night of the full moon, usually three months after the circumcision, a feast is held by the entire community. Songs of courage, bravery, and stamina are sung as the boys stomp dance in their line formation. The fathers place garlands of leaves and feathers around their son's necks as a symbol of pride and then join the line dance formed by the rest of the fathers. Even though the festivities continue for a lengthy time, the young men are escorted to their huts to prepare for the hunt beginning at dawn.

As the festivities close down, the fires are left to burn in order to be ready for the hunter's kill. The young men enter the jungle in intervals, traveling in twos. Armed with a spear, bow and arrow and/or knife, they dash forward to bring in the prized game, which may be birds, monkeys, or wild pigs. They each need to kill only one animal or fowl in order to return to the village compound triumphantly. It is during the year of a young man's seventeenth or eighteenth birthday that he is sent out alone to kill the mighty lion with his spear. This level of initiation quickly determines his physical prowess and, above all, his courage. All that he has been taught, everything he has observed and experienced will be put to the ultimate test for survival. Of course, this method of creating a warrior is not practiced by too many tribes; however, a young man must prove his hunting capabilities with a mighty kill. Yet there are tribes that will send the young man on a survival mission for six months to a year, in which time he will soon discover who he is and will be. It is a time for him to commune with the nature of all things that have been created by the powerful and sacred deities. This "vision quest" is still practiced by many people of all faiths and creeds. The time spent on these warrior quests is usually three to seven days at a time.

When a young man returns to his home after surviving in the immense unfamiliar forest, he is greeted with honor and pride. He is now a man, a warrior. He will tell his many perilous adventures for years to come. And most of them will be true. He will tell his stories of challenge, bravery, and creativity in order to survive. He will sing of his loneliness at that time, his apprehensions of not knowing what would happen even in the next hour; he will continue with the revelations of the ancestors and the guidance by the deities. He now knows that survival was not the major issue but that his awareness and relationship with the universe was far more important than just his being alive. Because of these experiences, he is indeed appreciative and understanding of life itself. He returns to his home secure in his choice of being a hunter/gatherer, a medicine man or a man ready to explore the outside world. The celebration begins.

The young girls facing this particular initiation do not fare quite so well as the young men, especially physically and emotionally. This initiation must be completed at puberty, perhaps between the tenth and twelfth years of age. The elder women of the village do it only once a year during the first day of the full moon.

The young girls are gathered in the center of the village compound encircled by all the females in the village. Songs, chants, and a stomp dance are performed until the elder breaks the circle and starts the procession to a secret place in the forest. All the girls and the women follow in line as the men have disappeared into their homes or wherever men go when they don't want to know what's really going on.

Once the sacred site is reached, the singing stops, and the initiation begins immediately. Her mother and other female relatives who have vivid memories of their own ordeal accompany the first young girl. The now-frightened young girl is held tightly by the arms and legs as the elder woman kneels between her legs. With a rapid thrust, the razor blade slices away the clitoris of the young girl. As the blood spurts out, the screaming child is doused with cold water. She is still held tightly whilst the elder woman applies the herbal poultice and leaves. The half-limp body of the child is carried to another hut to lie still until the pain subsides. Soon, the hut is filled with bleeding, crying, frightened young girls. Unfortunately, many times, the razor blade, scissors, or sharpened stone is very old and extremely dull and rusty. Regardless of the outcome, the initiation rites, as old as the tribes themselves, are still practiced to this day. Often, the outcome would be infection, excruciating pain, and even death, as some girls would bleed to death. Every woman must be circumcised. If not, then she is neither clean nor complete and will never be acceptable for marriage and childbirth. This belief is so imbedded within the psyche of these tribal women; there is never a question of the necessity for this tragic initiation.

Women who have taken up residence in other countries will always journey back home with their young daughters to receive this necessary initiation. Recently, it has become known throughout the Western world, and actions to cease this ritual have become the focal point of women worldwide. Interestingly enough, there are hospitals willing to circumcise the young girls under hygienic conditions with anesthesia. There have not been too many parents to accept the invitation; they choose to stay within the tradition of proper initiation by the elders and not by strangers who do not understand or respect their traditions. The status of education, wealth, or living far from their homeland is never an issue in the decision of going home for this ritual. It is widely known that the tribesmen will not marry or have sexual relationships with an uncircumcised woman no matter what. Many parents anguish over the necessity of continuing the tradition with their young daughters, but their belief that their daughters would be unfit to marry without being circumcised causes them to return for the initiation.

One of the many reasons given for this painful ordeal is that the clitoris is seen as a penis and is capable of destroying a man who has sex with a woman who has one. The clitoris is a demon put there by the gods to protect a woman's virtue. Only before her menses (bleeding) has started is the clitoris allowed to be removed and must be removed, or she will never be involved with family and tribe until she commits to being circumcised. Another belief is that an uncircumcised woman is more virile and stronger than a man because she is possessed by a devil, and she is quite capable of killing a man in agony and ecstasy. To add to the list of beliefs is that any man who has sex with an uncircumcised woman is in reality having sex with another man and that is the greatest taboo.

Regardless of how barbaric the civilized communities make this initiation, the African communities are not the only practitioners in the world. The creation of the castrati, young boys castrated before puberty, in Europe was widely accepted to preserve the operatic qualities of the young boys' voices. The castration of these children was carried out in the same blunt manner as the circumcision rituals of Africa. These young boys had no choice in the decision to be castrated; their high soprano voices were regarded with much more honor and pride than their ability to procreate.

Even though creating castrati is not practiced today, the fact remains that it was done by a society that considered themselves to be of the civilized world. Castration did not exist under the guise of religion, customs, or tradition; it existed for entertainment only. Justification for any act of body mutilation lies with the believer and the community that sanctions the ordeal.

The first "bleeding" of a young girl (the onset of menstruation) is usually a painful and terrifying experience for her. The young girl is whisked away from the community to be settled in a shelter outside of the home that she gets to know well until her "bleeding" has ceased. A spot on the stones or the bare ground is chosen to receive this "bleeding," usually under a sacred tree or in a sacred grotto. Three times a day, she rises to bury the "bleeding" by covering it with dirt, or she must bury the small stone upon which she was sitting. She bathes herself with a solution of leaves and water; after which, she moves to another spot to repeat the process. During the night, she makes a padding of leaves to place between her legs as she sleeps. In the morning, the used leaves are buried, and then she bathes herself with the herbal mixture of leaves and water. The young girl's mother or family members bring her food to eat as well as changes of clothing if necessary. This "bleeding" time is a meditative time for her, yet she must endure the pain of cramps, and usually, the duration of time is seven days or more, depending on the healing level of her circumcision. Because many communities insist on the vulva of the young girl to be sewn tightly, the menstrual blood can only seep out, causing a back up of blood in the uterus, which is extremely painful.

Meanwhile, she must follow the protocol that has been set forth for generations. The young girl's mother will often give her certain leaves to chew that will dull the pain and thin the blood for easier passage. Not much is explained to the young girl as to what is happening to her; it is an accepted way of life preparing her for the future as a grown woman, as future mother, as a healer, as a wife, as a worthy member of her village. Now is the time for her to show courage and strength; now is the time for her to take her place in the society as a grown woman. She is no longer a little girl full of play.

It has been a long and difficult struggle for women to release the old and traditional ways of initiation, and the most adamant foes for this needed change are the women themselves. Worldwide activity for the abolishing of such practices as female circumcision still rages on, yet the practice continues throughout the African diaspora. Exposure of these practices by way of books and films has made some headway; they have caught the attention of many groups who are attempting to bring about a change in the practice of circumcision of women.

It is important to remember the intense belief of African women that female circumcision is necessary in order to gain husbands has come from the practice of a long, long line of women. Unfortunately, this barbaric and unjust ritual is perpetuated by the male population. Fortunately, there are several movements sponsored by the Western world to abolish this female punishment. There is some progress, but as of this very moment there are still secret rituals of female circumcision. All of us can relate to faith, belief, and tradition, but to be blind and closed to other options is a sad commentary on religion as we know it.

To butcher and torture young girls for the sake of initiation is hardly worth their scarred bodies, minds, and spirits. It is hardly worth their death from unclean tools that are considered safe because they are regarded as sacred relics. Women are guilty for this abominable procedure, and women must rise up together and rid the entire world of this practice.

Chapter 4

Preface

I made it! Through all the anxieties, doubts, fears, I made it through the age of twelve. So I decided that I wanted to start my teen years with a bang. Nothing short of a formal ball would be accepted. I designed the invitations and had them printed up by the neighborhood printer. I reserved the local playground hall, and from the neighborhood night club, I borrowed tables and chairs. The night club owner even contributed the local club band to play the music (I was preparing to play phonograph records).

Everybody at school received an invitation to my thirteenth birthday party and were they excited, as was I. I thought of everything, and as luck would have it, I found a beautiful blue evening gown in the secondhand store. As soon as I told the clerk about my upcoming ball, she gave me the dress. It fit me perfectly. She also found the perfect shoes for the gown; they were a bit small, but I was used to feet that hurt.

Three days before my birthday ball, a mother of one of my "guests" met my mother in a store and asked if her daughter could wear a short gown to the party. I was not prepared for the reaction of my entire family when I finally got home from school.

Can you believe that in all of the planning and plotting, I never asked permission to do this from anybody? I completely forgot that I needed permission to do anything in my life. Well, the ball was canceled, and nobody spoke to me at school the following Monday. I was given a thirteenth birthday party at my house on the same day as the scheduled ball, and nobody came, except for Charlie, my childhood friend. This was not the rite of passage that I dreamed of.

Nevertheless, I would later become aware that there were many traditions that acknowledge the transitions that each person experiences.

The Ritual Of Manhood and Womanhood

Every tradition has a different time set for reaching adulthood. Whether the age is reached to earn a driver's license or to vote in public elections, or for drinking of alcohol or for legal marriage, the community law decides what that proper age will be. There is always some form of acknowledgment to mark and identify this most important transition. This is a time of great pride and honor for the young candidate as well as for the families. As with all traditions, this coming of a certain age requires various responsibilities and "tests" to prove the candidate's worthiness. There is always an air of excitement and great expectations surrounding the village compound as these young men and women prepare to enter "real life," and they can hardly wait. This type of initiation can hardly be compared to a coming-out party or a birthday or even a graduation party because of the severity, both physical and mental, of the initiation. Yet every young woman and young man eagerly awaits the start of the ceremonies, knowing that at the end, they will be recognized and accepted as the warriors of the village.

The elders will gather together in the center of the village to announce the names of the candidates. The villagers will form a circle around the elders and the young people. Usually, the first ritual is for the young men only. There is a very strong tradition in most African tribes, not all by any means but most, that men must be first at all times. The women may watch and sing along with the men as the men form straight lines to begin the songs along with the drumbeats.

Because this is a major ceremony, the finest regalia is worn by everyone—feathers, beaded necklaces, armbands, ankle bands, waist bands, the shells worn in the hair and around the neck, fabric of the same design and color (i.e., the complete costume that was worn by the ancestors). The songs tell the history of the village, the good times and the bad times, the deities, the gods and the goddesses, and above all, the ancestors. The songs spell out quite clearly the responsibilities of these youth to their village, their family, and their ancestors. Their line dance has been performed the same way for hundreds of years, and they are instructed never to change it.

The singing and dancing and drumming continue for hours, reaching a level of exultation and fatigue. Soon, the medicine man instructs the boys to lie flat on their backs in a straight line, while the adult men stomp their feet rhythmically to the drumbeat all around them. The younger men can hardly breathe.

The medicine man kneels at the top of the first boy's head. This boy is usually the son or grandson of the leader of the village; next in line would be the boys of the elder's family. As the medicine man kneels, he raises his sharpened stone in a salute to the ancestors and the deities. With a quick move, the medicine man cuts three marks on each cheek in a pattern that identifies the village or tribe to which they belong. The wounds are covered with a black poultice that will allow them to heal but to keep the pattern. Each boy goes through the same process without flinching or showing any signs of pain or fear. When the marking has been completed on all of the young men, they are pulled up by the circle of men to join them in the stomping dance.

This night, these young initiates will sleep together in a special place that is sacred to the village. It might be a tree, a boulder, or on the banks of a river. The sleep is for a few hours only because the next phase of the initiation starts at sunrise.

Food is served to the boys at dawn, and a pouch of berries, wheat cakes, and protection charms is given to each of them by their families. Protection charms are always worn by everyone and believed to ward off evil spirits, bad luck, and curses that could be brought on by other people. These protection charms are made solely by the medicine man who concocts various items according to the person's circumstances. The term "ju-ju bag" is understood by the villagers to be a protection charm. The medicine man uses dried entrails from some fowl or animal, certain berries, leaves or bark from a magical tree, pebbles from a sacred tree, powder or dust from ground herbs to make up a protective charm. On this particular initiation, the family usually requests that the medicine man make a protective charm for their child's initiation. This to keep their child safe from anything evil and to make him successful with the initiation. The boys gladly wear them.

The boys now pray to the ancestors to guide and protect them on their hunt. Armed only with their bows and arrows that each boy made previously, they walk into the forest one by one to face whatever the gods have in store for them. They are expected to return to the village by nightfall with their kill. Each must hunt a small animal or bird with his arrow remaining in the kill to prove that he and no other was the hunter. Many boys prefer using their homemade sling shots, but the elders insisted they must use the bow and arrow as did the ancestors. The boys can only travel in twos or alone. Once they return, they must clean and prepare the game for cooking in which the entire village will share. A pit in the ground is readied with hot coals and hot stones, the game is wrapped in leaves and placed in the pit and then covered with large leaves. There may be yams and other vegetables added to complete the feast. When all of the young men have returned and the meat and vegetables cooked, the drums begin, and the songs of victory and warriorship heighten the pride of the villagers. The young men dance to show off their prowess and cunning. The young girls are delightfully impressed. The "party" moves into high gear and usually goes on for hours even after all the food is eaten.

In present day, the honor of the warrior is determined by what the young man brings back to the village in the form of "the kill." Today, the kill can be represented by his worldly achievements. This may include a degree from a university, a successful business, or becoming a sports hero or politician; any accomplishment that can translate into prosperity or abundance for his village. In whatever form "the kill" manifests, the young warrior is always recognized with the highest honor of the village, with the acknowledgment and celebration of the warrior's return.

As with all communities, some young men leave and never return. It is then that he is declared dead to the ancestors, and only upon his return with his "kill" will he be "alive to the ancestors" and duly acknowledged. It is remembered that the ancestors lost young men to animal attacks who never returned to the village; therefore, these young warriors were declared dead to the ancestors. However, the psychological drive to return home is often enough to force the young warrior to return home no matter how long he has been away. The tribal ties are not easy to break no matter how sophisticated the young warrior becomes. The ancestral demands are much stronger than the will of the youth. He knows that he must answer the call to return. He is not allowed to forget and abandon or he will be forever haunted even to the point of misfortune and mishap. The young warrior dares not ignore his commitment to the ancestors, his family, his elders, and his village. This deep desire to return home is the cornerstone of the survival of the village and the ancestors. Nothing in the world is more important or satisfying than to honor the ancestors because he, the young warrior, knows that one day, he too will be an ancestor.

In as much as the focus has been on the making of the warrior, the rites of passage for the young woman do play an important role in the community. As expected, the elder women control the activities of bringing the young girl into her place of womanhood. The events for this occasion are not always as dramatic as the young warriors', but they are deemed just as necessary. Again, the ages vary from village to village, but the main events of a "first bleeding" and "circumcision" are the spearheads of the initiation into womanhood. The fanfare is rather subtle and certainly more subdued than for the boys. Usually, only the women of the compound are involved with these special rites, calling on the men at the very end to hunt for the feast and to beat the drums at the ceremonies. Oddly enough, women are forbidden to beat the drums because their legs cannot ever enclose the drums. This would expose their genitals to the spirit of the drums.

It has been said that the deities and the supreme creator decreed all of the customs and laws governing the well-being of and attitudes for women. It was not the men who designed their rituals, their dress codes, their behavior for marriage, their attitudes for rearing children, nor their responsibilities to the family, home, and community. The gods and the ancestors take great pride in having women follow strict guidelines of worship, work, and family. It is said that those who have not been born and raised with the gods and the ancestors would never understand or believe in the disciplines set forth for their people. As a result of their lack of understanding and lack of respect, these unknowing persons would try to bring change and disorder to the devotees, thereby creating chaos in order for the people to abandon and destroy the foundation of African life.

The re-enactment of the initiation ceremonies must be exact and as elaborate as can be afforded. Change is not an issue for the women who are participating fully in the customs and culture of their ancestors. However, change has become an issue brought on by contact with the outside world.

Women's rituals are still strict and sometimes volatile because of the differences of opinion, but the effort is made, and eventually, the ritual is completed.

Mothers are joyous to offer their daughters into womanhood for many reasons; not the least of which is to receive the blessings from the gods and ancestors for preserving a way of life and for sacrificing so much to raise a daughter. A mother knows that her daughter must have a decent dowry by the time she is ready to be married. If the mother is poor, then any acquisition for the dowry is a hardship, and something for the family must be left out. No matter how many daughters are in the family, each one must have a dowry at the time of her marriage. Even if the family is wealthy, a mother starts her daughter's training for womanhood by preparing the dowry for marriage.

The beginning of the ritual is the young women's physical cleansing which is usually held at the river, or water is carried to the compound by the younger girls. If the ceremony begins at the river, the elder must determine when they, the young women, will be able to enter the river because if the gods or spirits are bathing they must not be disturbed or looked upon while they bathe. Once this time is agreed upon by the elder women, the young women are given the signal to run to the river in silence and jump in, submerging their entire bodies for at least one minute. Leaves from a sacred tree are used by the elder women to scrub every part of each young woman's body; after which, she is pushed under the water again for one minute. This scrubbing is done three times. Any woman, young or old, who has her "bleeding" time is not allowed to participate, nor are they allowed to be anywhere near the vicinity of the ritual. The "bleeding" women are kept away from the village, and all rituals and ceremonies until they are finished and may safely return to the compound.

Once the young women are bathed, they kneel at the river's edge to offer prayers to the deities and the ancestors. Songs and chants of praise and thanks are enthusiastically sung while they stomp and dance in a circle. Large leaves are spread out on the riverbank for each girl. Then the elders bless them. Each girl lies on her back when told by the elder medicine woman, forming a straight line of naked bodies on leaves. The elder medicine woman removes the sharp stone or razor (usually rusted) from her medicine bag, raises it above the head of the first young woman, softly chanting incantations from ancient times. Two deep cuts are made between the eye and the ear on both sides of the face. The medicine woman continues the same process with each girl as each mother, aunt, or grandmother fills each cut with the herbal mixture to stop the bleeding yet keeping the wound opened. The young girls are given a bitter herbal drink or bitter leaves to chew which lessen the pain and calm the nerves. They are put down to sleep in the sacred grove that has been prepared beforehand. The mothers and families sing old songs through the night.

It is at this time that the grandmothers of each young woman will teach them about sex. The mothers, aunts, cousins, and close friends will later teach them about the responsibilities of being a wife, a mother, and tending to the gardens, as well the household chores. Even though these young women have been trained to the duties of gardening, milking the goats, bringing water, gathering firewood, and taking care of their younger siblings, they must know how to build the family dwelling and how to take it down if necessary to move to another location. They must know how to make the earthenware pots for cooking and weave the mats for covering the huts. During this womanhood initiation, she is strongly reminded and retaught the moral codes for a woman that wants to stay in the good graces of the community. She knows that the ancestors are depending on her to preserve the culture of the tribe by being the nurturer of the family. For thirty to forty days, she goes through secret rituals and serious lecturing on the pitfalls of womanhood. She is warned repeatedly about staying a virgin until married. She will be ostracized for being barren since that is a definite punishment by the deities. She is commanded to always keep the sacred shrines in her home up to standard. She is screamed at to always obey her husband because he is the head and the leader of the family. She is reminded to teach her daughters the ways of the ancestors, and above all, she must swear to keep secret the rituals that she has seen and in which she has participated. The young woman understands that her daughters are her responsibility to teach and train; however, her husband is the absolute authority over her sons. She is instructed that her husband is the disciplinarian, yet he must not be abusive to her or to her children. If he is violent, then she is to report him to her family; after which, the elders of the village will administer some form of punishment in order for him to correct his ways.

When this rite of passage into womanhood is completed and the mothers are satisfied with the outcome, the entire group returns to the village to announce that their daughters are now ready for marriage. She is a woman, even though she may only be fifteen or sixteen years of age.

The celebration begins with all of the women and young girls of all ages dancing, singing, and preparing feast food. This is a major occasion for the entire village because the tribal bloodlines will be ongoing.

The solemn oath taken by each young woman and each young man at these particular rites is that no matter where they go and no matter what they do; they must always return to the village to honor their parents as well as to pay homage to the ancestors. Not to return means the dismissal from the tribe and losing their names. Very few will dishonor their parents and their ancestors.

The rituals of adulthood are the most important for young men and women, as it means they now have the freedom from their parents' dominance, as it is with every teenager who reaches that golden age of twenty-one. These young people will now make decisions for themselves and will also be responsible for those decisions. Yet regardless of how old they may become, they can never disrespect their parents. Many of the young women will go immediately into marriage and motherhood, others will leave to attend boarding school if they have been educated in previous years. The young men will often stay in the village to build their own huts to prepare for marriage, or they too will leave for further education or other opportunities. All of them approach this new level with dreams, hopes, and excitement to do better than their parents. But above all, whatever they do is to please the ancestors.

During initiation rituals, amidst the celebration, the elders often sing stories that encourage these "new heads" to remain in their villages and avoid the "false life" outside of their compound; they sing of the great prosperity and of the abundance of their harvests that will come to pass if they do not leave the village. Yet the elders know deep within their souls that these young men and women have been taught how to read, and they want more. Life is no longer the simple existence it once was for the ancestors. Their initiation ceremonies have resulted in a deeper change and a greater shift in their psyche: they must leave, they must explore, they must challenge, they must see what is beyond the forests. They are no longer just tribesmen. They are adults; their initiation makes them so.

These "new heads" remind their parents as well as the elders of the village that once, the ancestors were forced to leave the village as slaves, but they kept the religion and the customs as best they could. But now, when they, the "new heads," leave the village of their own free will, they will promise the elders of their intent to honor the ancestors properly and support the village as best they can. They speak of the ancestors that now exist over the entire world. And even though they may adopt the religion of their new land, they will always be reminded of their roots and the commitments to their customs and traditions. They promise not only to teach their children the ways of the elders but to return to the village with their children for the established initiations.

The "new heads" are warned not to forget the ancestors or to forego the traditions—Africa is changing, but the soul of Africa can never change. This is the initiation of adulthood that bears the oath of allegiance to the ancestors and Africa. The celebration is festive and sad at the same time—festive for those who will leave as adults, and sad for those who no longer have "children." Handcrafted mementos and charms for protection are prepared by both of the parents and the medicine man, and many times, the chief and the elders of the village will create a gift that is filled with powerful magic.

Chapter 5

Preface

Just as the baby chicks are pushed out of the nest, so are the young people of twenty-one years by every tradition. Usually, it's much sooner, but we were allowed to stay until twenty-one, and after that, we were told to "let the door knob hit you in the back!" It was a great time for the parents as well as for those who made it to adulthood in one piece. The parents were no longer responsible for you or to you, both by law and by tradition. Hooray! This definitely called for a celebration to finally reach that golden age of twenty-one. Actually, that day for me was no different than the day before and the day after. I was in college at that time and studying for finals.

What a rude awakening was that day of independence for me. Because my family never trained me or even discussed with me how to handle money, bills, and most of all life; I was handicapped from the outset.

What I must not forget is that no one trained them either. This was it—my detachment from rules, regulations, and best of all, my parents' long arms of control. This was no dress rehearsal. I knew how to cook, how to clean a house, and how to keep myself clean. Above all, never ask your family for money. You either sank or swam. The final words were, "So, you wanna be grown . . ."

The Rites of Independence

The making of an "adult" is not usually determined by age or size; rather, it is marked by the number and the types of previous initiations. This particular rite takes on a different energy and form from the secret initiations that they have endured. The entire village gathers food that will serve everyone. New tribal clothes are made by each young woman and each young man who is to be a celebrant. The young women may shave their heads or have a friend "do their new head" in a beautiful complex pattern which may take two or three days to complete. New skirts are made of beads, fabric, and/or grass. The men gather feathers, beads, animal skins, animal teeth, and various kinds of small shells. Everyone must be beautiful, and they are.

Each celebrant brings a handcrafted gift to the parents, elders, and above all, the ancestors. Usually, the young women will present a cooking pot or some utensil for the preparation of food or a necklace of beads, shells or elephant hair, or even bones from sacrificed animals. The young men will fashion swords or spears or bows and arrows; also, the young men will make elaborate headdresses and fantastically carved masks and sometimes, carved objects which are presented as sacred gifts to the ancestors if the young man intends to be a master carver. Other young men may choose to make a ceremonial drum, which is always useful; however, to present a ceremonial drum requires a separate ceremony that is conducted by the village healer and the elders. These drums require intricate markings that will symbolize the magical power that has been instilled through dance and song and incantations. The ceremony of the drum forms the link from the present back to the ancestors. The drum now has a soul and is able to "speak"; however, not just anyone is allowed to "beat" the drum, nor is a woman allowed to take on the drum. Initiation of the drummer starts at an early age, and then the drum must chose the candidate. This ceremony binds the drummer's soul to the soul of the drum, and they become as one.

Just as the sun begins to fade into evening, the drummers begin a slow steady rhythm that has been used for centuries in order to call the people to gather in the center of the village. The initiates remain in their houses until called forth by the village elders. Along with local neighbors and visitors, family members from other towns return for this auspicious ceremony. There is much laughter, plenty of food, and plenty of children. The women and children form on one side and the men and boys form on the other side. The village elders sit "at the head" between the sexes. Everyone is excited and looking forward to a gala evening of food, dance, and drink.

Suddenly, there is a loud shout from the village chief; the people respond with just as loud a shout which says, "What?" The chief shouts out twice more, receiving the same response with laughter. Now the chief becomes serious, he rises, walks to the center of the circle; he faces east and starts the invocation of the ancestors. Everyone listens quietly. The fire is started by the medicine man who has already prepared the ingredients that will be necessary for an all-night ritual.

The drums begin a rhythm that is a sharp-sounding slow cadence; the men begin a short side-step shuffle, keeping a close-knit large circle around the medicine man and the fire. The drums beat stronger and louder and faster, and the men grunt louder and side-step faster; they add a quick hunching movement of their shoulders as they move to the strong drumbeat.

Now begins a strange twist in this ceremony of introduction to adulthood. The candidates are ushered into the center of the circle and begin the side-step dance as the men are doing. The medicine man gathers hot ashes into a gourd that is now smoldering heavy and thick fumes. Each candidate is held by the arms and shoulders by two men and is raced to the fuming gourd. The candidate is pushed to his knees, and his head is held over the fumes for a few seconds. His head is yanked backwards and thrust back into the fumes. This inhalation is completed after seven times; the candidate is carried away to his hut because he is unable to move. Each candidate will have their own gourd containing the ritual leaves. After the last candidate has been deposited in their respective huts, the "real" party starts with eating, drinking, singing, and dancing until the sun begins to rise and everyone begins to filter toward their huts. There are always a few left to make sure there is no drink left or food uneaten. The fire is left to burn out, and the village is silent.

Upon waking, the candidates usually feel quiet, subdued, and somewhat lethargic. They seem to know that they have been through something, but they are not quite sure exactly what. They do know that they are now official adults, ready to be an integral part of the village; they now have a voice that will be heard and respected. They no longer need the permission of parents, elders, family, or medicine man to do whatever they choose. It is a wonderful, awesome, and happy time in their lives.

Chapter 6

Preface

I don't remember hearing the words "I love you" as a child. If you had clothes, food to eat, and a roof over your head, you were loved. Every family that I knew expressed love through what they gave you throughout your life. I could not understand why people got married. Often, they would be so angry with each other and fight each other like gladiators or ignore each other at any time and any place and still stay together.

Marriage is still a mystery to me because it is a tradition that will never go away, and a tradition that is, it seems, necessary to God. I believe that if someone would research this phenomenon of marriage deeply and extensively, I'll bet they will discover some amazing and startling facts that would make this ritual needless.

Our nations, our governments, our laws, rules, and regulations, our sense of purpose and direction are based on the ritual of marriage. Since I eloped, I never quite felt married, but the union, real or not, lasted until death did us part.

I must admit, the romantic preparation for a marriage is the ritual itself. The invitations, the wedding gown, the church or wedding site all make up the ritual and the "binding" for however long. The expenses are phenomenal, and the show is pure entertainment with all the tears and all the laughs, and they live happily ever after—right! I never questioned the ritual of marriage until now, and I still don't know the answer. But somewhere deep inside of me, I believe that when we are given the truth about this ritual, we all are going to be shocked. But until then, let the ceremony begin.

If we took a long hard look at this modern-day ritual of marriage, perhaps a different reality needs to be brought forth. For example, the wedding gown—long, flowing, white, virginal, and to be worn only once in this lifetime; the veil that mysteriously covers the face and can only be removed by the father; the bridal bouquet that is carried precociously by the bride somewhere along the pelvic area; and the question of, "Who gives this woman away?" "I do," replies the father and literally places her hand into the hands of her intended. Are you beginning to get the real picture? The presents and family members of each sit on opposite sides of the marriage area. Note that the father of the bride pays for everything because that is part of the dowry he must pay for having a daughter.

The Secret Rites of Marriage

The bonding of a man and woman in marriage in African tradition acknowledged a broader concept than a Christian marriage. The word "love" never entered the equation; the elders and the parents of all children arranged the who and the when. Perhaps it could be understood why fathers were always elated to have sons instead of daughters. Daughters required expensive and expansive dowries in order to marry. Some fathers remained in debt for their entire lifetime because of their daughter's dowry. A dowry means that the woman's father presented to the prospective groom's father an array of gifts of cattle, food, rare shells, hand-woven fabric, farming tools, and, if it were at all possible, some form of money.

Long discussions between families are presided over by the elders, and sometimes, it would take several months, even a year or more, to settle the question of the size of the dowry.

No matter how poor a family may be, they must have a dowry in order for their daughter to marry. Since marriage was a family matter, the dowry gifts would be made by all the family's women, and the family's men would gather the seeds for planting, the feathers from the birds of the forest, as well as shells that most likely were passed from generation to generation. However, if a family had a wealthy status, they would be expected to give precious and expensive jewels consisting of gold and silver, as well as farm land, and even personal gifts to every family member. This could be tobacco, certain foods, alcoholic beverages, sweets, and fine cloth.

Once the marriage contract had been approved by both the families and the date had been set by the elders and the medicine man, preparations would start. The father of the bride-to-be would be the overseer, and he was quite strict in order to avoid embarrassment before the villagers.

Invitations would be sent out by way of drumbeating or messenger. Many times, the prospective bride will walk for miles, escorted by her young girl friends, going from village to village, making the happy announcement of her forthcoming marriage. Of course, gifts are expected since this is the method used to start the couple in their new life. The custom of gift giving is an ancient tradition that is a belief of sharing and tithing to support a person's worthiness. The gifts will consist of clay pots for carrying water as well as cooking, hand-woven baskets used for storage of food as well as for carrying fruits and vegetables, hand-woven fabric to be worn for special ceremonial times, and all types of food and drink to add to the celebration. Again, the status of the family will determine the quality of the gift.

The entire village will participate in the activities of the upcoming marriage ceremony. New clothes are woven, elaborate headdresses are shaped and decorated. Many shells and handmade beads are strung for necklaces, armbands, and bracelets for the wrists and ankles as well as for the waists. The men begin the long task of preparing their favorite fermented brew.

It is imperative that the bride is a virgin; otherwise, the family of the groom will regard her as tainted and will refuse the marriage, which they often do. Therefore, the women elders will accompany the bride-to-be to a secret place in the forest to make sure that she has learned the ways of being a wife and mother and, of course, to examine her for her virginity. It is at this time that the young bride-to-be must have her circumcision tight and in good order. If the circumcision is in need of repair because the young girl is no longer a virgin, then the agony starts all over again with the sewing together of the labia. This is kept in strict secrecy between the family women.

The family believes that she, the bride-to-be, needs to suffer for having sex before she married. After making sure that the young woman has proficient skills for her new family, the women return to the village with loud celebration. The village joins the festive group, and the wedding plans continue.

The day of the wedding starts early in the morning with dressing and adorning the young bride. About noon, the groom arrives to escort the bride to the village elders. He is accompanied by his friends—all young men dressed in their warrior garb. The bride veils her head and face with a headpiece made of shells. The families will arrive later. The medicine woman and man bring them inside the hut in order to receive blessings and permission from the ancestors to marry. Just as a matter of interest, no ancestor has ever said no to a marriage, that I know of.

Inside the hut, the medicine man collects spittle and urine from the couple in order to make a poultice for the ensuing ceremony. The medicine man instructs the couple to lie flat on their backs, side by side, on the dirt floor. Chants are started to invoke the deities and the ancestors to drive out any evil and negative forces that wish to destroy this union. As the chant rises to a fervent pitch, the medicine man drinks an herbal solution and sprays the couple with a fine mist from his mouth. This action is repeated three more times. The couple is told to turn over on their stomachs, and the spraying blessing is performed four times, from head to feet. A smudging of fine powder is blown over each of them—front and back. The couple is told to stand but not to touch each other. Upon rising, the young man is blindfolded.

It has always been believed that a man and woman should honor and acknowledge the ancestors with particular sacred actions to announce their matrimony. There is a secret rite performed by the elders and the medicine man and medicine woman. Public rites are witnessed by the entire village and invited guests.

The dowry is one of the most important aspects of the entire ceremony. Usually, a dowry has been associated only with females giving extensive gifts and money to her prospective husband and his family. However, the dowry ritual is practiced by the bride and groom; it is a fair exchange in order for them to begin their life together. The goal of this union is to procreate in order to always honor the ancestors and to sustain the village. Love does not enter into this marriage agreement; what is important is how many children will be born to carry on the traditions of hunting, farming, and protection.

During the secret rite of marriage, the young woman or girl must endure her husband using a knife or sharpened stone to cut open the stitches that were applied to close her labia during her circumcision ritual. She is held down by the medicine woman while the elders and medicine woman gather around her husband who has been prepped for this deed. Ancestral songs and chants are sung to deafen any screams from the bride. As soon as the opening has been completed, herbs and ash are applied to the area to stop the bleeding and to hasten the healing. Large leaves are used to bind the area between her legs because she must continue with the public ceremony. (Once the bleeding has been stemmed, the bride is given a strong herbal drink that will deaden the pain and settle her anxiety.) She is later dressed for the public ceremony with the adornment of beads, shells, and feathers. She is painted with symbols on her arms, legs, and face. Even though the bride is woozy from the strong drink, she makes her appearance with her husband for the villagers. Upon the couple's entrance, shrills and drums begin enthusiastically to escort them to their seats of honor.

The urine that was previously collected from the couple, the medicine man pours from his vessel to the ground. The husband then walks and stamps in it until the urine has disappeared. The same thing is done for the bride, even though the women must assist her. All of the elders must check the ground to be sure nothing is left. Having completed the ground search, it is loudly announced that the ancestors have given their approval for this union. The medicine man approaches the couple with a sacred vine with which he ties the couple's wrists. That officially binds them together as husband and wife.

The merriment continues, but the couple is led away by their friends and family to their new home. The husband cannot have any type of sexual relations with his new wife. He must wait for seven nights; after which, he may do as he wishes.

Because tradition has prepared both of them, none of these actions come as a surprise. It is necessary, and it is wanted by them. Meanwhile, the young bride is tended by her family during the day, and the husband is cared for by his family. Once the marriage has been consummated, the couple returns to the elders to receive their blessings and official recognition. Immediately, they settle into their married life.

When problems arise, and they do, the couple reports the incident to the elders. Many problems arise from extreme expectations on both sides. Often, the quality of meals and the preparations required are not to the liking of the husband. The wife contends that the husband has never had proper food; therefore, he can't recognize what is good and what is not good.

Such problems as readiness for sex, time spent with friends and family, poor housekeeping, as well as not obeying her husband are usually the complaints brought against the bride. Whereas the bride complains that he is domineering and lazy, he is a bad hunter, he is critical of all that she does, and above all, he does not function well during the sex act.

The elders do resolve many of these conflicts, and many couples do work through their problems, especially when she becomes pregnant. However, there are couples that do not make their marriage a success. For them, the answer is to dissolve the marriage with another secret and sacred ritual.

The elders make the final decision to divorce or not to divorce. But if the decision is to allow the divorce, the entire village is assembled, and the couple is placed in the center of the gathering. Whoever initiated the divorce will face the other, and at a given signal from the elder, three steps are taken backwards; after which, the other party takes three steps backwards. The initiator spits three times into the dirt, then the opposite party spits three times into the dirt. They cross-walk to each others' place, and with their left foot, they cover the spittle with dirt. The area is inspected by the elders, and then they declare the marriage is dissolved.

The woman leaves with her family to a secret place in order to have her labia sewn up again. If there are any children from the union, they accompany the mother, unless the boys have reached the age of five, in that case they must go with their father. There is no singing, drumming, dancing, or feasting.

For the couples who do have a successful marriage, the anniversaries are always celebrated by the village. These celebrations are not as grand as the wedding because of the expense, but the same enthusiasm is present. Oddly enough, after each childbirth, some women prefer to have their labia resewn in order to please their husbands upon resuming intercourse.

The ritual of marriage is not taken lightly or disrespected. The entire village lends support for the couple to understand their commitments to the ancestors; therefore, the couples do tend to stay together to raise their family in the traditional manner.

In other tribes, the wedding night belongs only to the husband and the wife who must perform a ritual of consummation. Even though the couple has had an enjoyable day, they realize what comes next. In the privacy of their house or hut, they begin to prepare for the final binding to each other. They both drink the herbal solution prepared by the medicine man that will relieve the agony of the cutting operation. The woman lies down on leaves that are covered with a piece of fabric that was designated as the wedding shroud. They pray to the ancestors and the deities for blessings and protection. Meanwhile, the potion begins to take effect. At this moment, the woman lies on the wedding bed, and the husband mounts her to begin penetration. If there is too much tight stitching from her circumcision, he must use his knife or cutting stone to make an opening. The husband continues the penetration until he has had completion. The wife administers the prepared herbs and leaves to her vaginal area. They both drink more of the herbal potion. In the morning, the husband takes the wedding shroud to the elders for their minute inspection to determine that it is his wife's blood and not animal blood. This inspection assures that the couple did not have sexual intercourse before the sacred rites. With the elder's satisfaction of the blood's authenticity, the couple announces to everyone that the marriage is bona fide. Then the drumming and festivities begin and lasts all day and all night. The couple does not attend; they are served all meals and drink for at least a week, sometimes longer. When they do emerge, they are regarded as any other member of the village.

If a bride has not been circumcised, the husband has every right to dissolve the marriage immediately. The men have been trained never to have sex with an uncircumcised woman; if they do, then they have had sex with another man. She is a demon that will drain him of his life, she is more of a man than he is, she is both a man and a woman, and she can satisfy herself, but she cannot procreate; therefore, she is an obscenity. Under the laws of the ancestors, she is not to be wedded to anyone until she completes the ritual of circumcision. No matter where any man or woman lives in the world, they must obey the law of circumcision. Their children must never be allowed to decide whether or not they want the ritual. This is a must; otherwise, they are not fit for marriage, nor will they be allowed to be married in the tradition. This is the law of the ancestors and the voice of the deities. There are to be no exceptions for any reason. Therefore, many tribespeople will bring their children from afar to honor that commitment.

In more ancient times, men used the term marriage to mean something totally different from what marriage means today. The meaning then was simply an acquisition branded with the man's mark. Kings, emperors, pharaohs, rulers of all kinds acquired territory, cattle, slaves, women, all goods, everything. When the woman was favored by the ruler, he would choose her to be closer to him in order to bear his children. Her title was wifedom, and she was branded symbolically with wearing a metal circle around her upper left arm (it was closest to her heart). If the female was a young child, the ruler would choose her to be in his wifedom when she started to bleed. The young girl would be given three metal bracelets to symbolize that she had been chosen to be in the wifedom of that ruler. The priests were able to give two bracelets for their choice, and one bracelet would be given by the common man. Decorations and symbols of who she belonged to were etched and carved into the bracelets.

The priests or the religious leader decided to develop a special ceremony to add to their long list of worship ceremonies. The priests believed that the more you involve people in a ceremony, the more you can control them, which, of course, would give the priests more power to rule. The ceremony was used to ensure the couple's faith in the priests, and the reward for doing this was to have an intensive celebration for acquiring his property (wife). The more wives you had proved how wealthy and virile you were. Thus, the tradition of the marriage ceremony and wedding vows took form, and many traditions soon became involved on some level of celebrating a man acquiring his property. To show everyone how important and wealthy he was, he would decorate his soon-to-be wife in fine fabrics, and he would present her in front of the priests to have them agree with his choice.

The man would add more decorated metal to his wives to brand them as his own. He used metal for the ears, fingers, toes, nose—anyplace that would hold the metal. No unmarried woman could wear metal if she had never been "acquired" (married). Only a man could give the "ring," and only women could wear them. The ruler became aware of the growing competition of the "rings" and decided he would have the largest and most beautiful ring of all, and only his wives would be able to wear them. He simply had an ornate necklace for his wives, each one different but beautiful. Of course, the wives loved it, and it soon became the fashion statement of all times.

The children of the union were "ringed" to the children of other men. The young girl would be draped in soft fabric from head to toe. No one should see her before she was "ringed" because any man could immediately choose her if she wore no rings. The father escorted his veiled daughter to the man who would "ring" her. Upon arriving at his home, the father would hand her over to the man who would immediately put the metal bracelet around her left arm. All of the men would take off to the priests to be blessed for acquiring. He blessed her to bear strong children. Thus, the ringing caused envy, and the priests took over and devised a new ceremony. The people didn't like sudden or complete change, so there was a compromise. The agreement was to be in a ritual with the priest in his sacred space and to bring his children for a vow of obedience to the gods. They could celebrate as much as they desired. But there would be no celebration just for acquiring. The birth of a son would be just cause for great celebration, whereas a girl would only be acquisition.

The son was an insurance for the future. And like any man, the more he has, the more he wants, and he loves the female.

This is a tale told by an old African shaman.

Chapter 7

Preface

I was just as fascinated by the word "magic" as everyone else. Pulling rabbits out of a hat, pouring milk into a newspaper funnel, or making things disappear was awesome to me (and still is). I soon discovered that there is a distinct and definite difference between magic and magick. Entertainment is not the objective for magick. The true focus for many magickal traditions is the supernatural and spiritual practices. Just as there are many beliefs, there are just as many types of magick, and they are seriously studied and taught by masters.

To many, magick is an art form designed to bring about change on some level to the practitioners. This change, albeit good or bad, from one thing to another, is regarded as a "miracle," almost spooky or scary. It is only when you delve into the world of spiritual magick does understanding occur.

Another name for magick is shamanism. It is the ability to communicate with all living life—plants, animals, insects, birds, reptiles, as well as spirits, entities, etc. Having this knowledge is regarded as being powerful and mighty.

Yet each of us perform some "magical" task each day without even knowing it.

In the following chapter, the "Shamanistic Magick," which is the foundation of all magic, both "stage magic" and "spiritual magick," will show the preparations for the journey of becoming a "miracle worker."

Initiation Into Magick

Magick has always been practiced in Africa. A relationship between the seen and the unseen requires specific talents and complex formulas that are traditionally passed from one generation to another by strict laws of initiation. The medicine man would choose the candidates based on interest in such things as well as a family's request to teach their child the way of the ancestors. Very often, a family member would dream of a child, who was a family member, being involved with the deities, the ancestors, and even surrounded by animals. Once this dream was reported, immediate action would be taken to identify which child it could be. The medicine man may have dreams signifying a young man or woman to be added to the initiate's ranks.

Once the candidate has satisfied the medicine man with payment or a promise to pay, as well as a keen interest in magick, then the necessary rituals are set in motion.

The philosophy or meaning of these ceremonies is usually kept secret. The initiate will endure rituals that he must never reveal to anyone. These sacred rites differ just as tribes and traditions differ, yet the common thread between all of them is the fact that some rite, ritual, and ceremony must be performed on all who choose to follow that path of magick and power.

The initiation rites that are shared here are common knowledge for anyone. Those activities that are omitted and not revealed at this time will not be missed.

With due respect, the format will remain, but the delicate details will remain hidden as promised.

Knowing how to work magick within the villages was necessary to protect the villagers from spirit demons, famine, disease, ancestor wrath, and any other negative energy that would afflict a human being. It was because of this skill that the medicine man gained higher status than the ruler, and he used that skill to have power over everyone. The villagers feared and revered the "magick" man, so much so that, eventually, his word became law by way of the ruler. The medicine man made himself indispensable to the ruler with his advice and directives from the spirit, deity, and ancestors.

To be chosen to be a candidate for initiation was an honor to the family, and they would obey all of the demands of the medicine man.

The first step is the spiritual oracles, such as shells, snake bones, stones with painted symbols that will symbolize the acceptance by the deities and/or the ancestors for the candidate to be brought into the secret mysteries. This specific consultation will map out the directions for the candidate to follow as well as explicit instructions for the medicine man. The candidate's age varies from six or seven years of age to forty or fifty years of age. The time is always determined by the deities and the ancestors. Regardless of age, the candidate must endure all of the initiatory rites that have been prescribed. Now begins the *kooshay* level of initiation into magickal powers.

There are specific times of the year that these particular rituals are performed. Baptismal rites, wedding rites, death rites are determined by time of death, birth, by astrological timing, or even by deity anniversaries. The rising and setting of the sun and/or moon is another determining factor, as well as rainy season, planting season, harvesting season, and the migration time of certain animals and birds. Using the English language, any month with the letter *r* within the spelling would not be the time to initiate into the mysteries.

Once the timing was approved, the initiate's protocol teaching would be the introduction to the *kooshay* ritual. For example, whenever a candidate approached a ruler, an elder or dignitary, such as another medicine man or woman, he must salute in the following manner: bend the right knee only to the ground, never both knees because to kneel down on both knees signified being put to death as well as enslavement. Bending down on one knee signifies respect as well as acknowledgment of being inferior. Every gesture had a definite meaning, and precision was required and expected. While bending on the right knee, both arms would fold across the chest, showing the hands to be flat on the shoulders. This gesture ensured there were no hidden weapons, as well as being the position of servitude. The candidate must never look the one saluted directly in the eyes; a lowered head, even while talking, assured that level of respect for the official that was being saluted.

The candidate must always start the clapping of hands whenever anyone entered their *kooshay* space and the clapping whenever they left the space. Regardless of how many people came or left, the candidate must clap the hands continually as in applause for a concert performance. This is another gesture of respect, acknowledgment, and status.

When the candidate enters into the *kooshay* hut, he or she will not be allowed to speak audibly, nor will he or she be allowed to leave the sacred space for anything until the entire initiation has been completed. The medicine man and his apprentices begin the ritual with a "mystical bath" using leaves from sacred trees and bushes as well as a combination of herbs that have been boiled for hours. Every part of the body from the top of the head to the bottom of the feet is bathed by the medicine man. No spot on the body is left untouched for fear that demons and bad spirits could hide there. The head is then shaved to receive the symbols of initiation by carving with a razor-sharp stone or a knife. When the bleeding has been stemmed, certain types of "spirit food," such as corn, wheat, small eggs, small fruit seeds, and sea shells, are placed on the top of the head carving, and the head is quickly wrapped tightly in a long gauze-type fabric that will be worn the entire time of the initiation process. If an egg should break or any of the "spirit food" begins to spoil, then the candidate is banned from further initiation because the Spirits do not approve of the candidate at this time. The candidate leaves in disgrace for his family and must find the way to appease the ancestral spirits and the village deities before reapplying. Another reason for dismissal is the "bleeding" time coming on while the young woman is in the throes of the initiation or a candidate becoming violently ill or even frightened. All are reasons for being dropped as an apprentice. No magickal secrets are ever revealed at this level of initiation for fear that the candidate may not achieve completion and stay true to their vow of secrecy. This level of the initiation process will last for five years until the next initiatory level is allowed to further teach the candidate.

Now that the "cleansing" has been completed and the "head has been opened," the candidate is given a loose long garment to wear until the last day of the seclusion which varies from seven to twenty-one to thirty-three days. During this time, the candidate must lay down on a bed of sacred tree leaves with a rugged rock for a pillow. The candidate never stands except to go to the toilet, and even then, this act is done within the confines of the *kooshay* space. It is an apprentice who comes to collect the used gourds or bush leaves; the candidate cannot leave the sacred space and must be quick to return to his prone position on the sacred leaves. If the candidate needs or wants anything, he must clap his hands (applaud) to attract the attending apprentice. He signs and gestures his needs or wants to the apprentice who will then service his needs. Remember that he must still applaud the apprentices entering and leaving. The candidate soon learns not to ask for too much too often.

Food is brought to the candidate's hut twice a day by the family but served by the apprentice. The candidate is allowed to sit up in order to applaud and then eat but must lie down again after eating. All of the food prepared by the family must be cooked according to the medicine man's instructions, such as one day, all the food prepared must not have any salt; the next day, no sugar or sweetness; the next day, heavy spices; another day, no white-colored food. Each day required specific foods for specific deities and specific ancestors. Only water and herbal teas prepared by the apprentice are allowed for drinking.

Very late at night, when the entire village would be asleep, the medicine man would quietly awaken the candidate, drape some fabric over him, and escort him out of the *kooshay* space, provided the area would be clear of any people since no one may see the candidate outside of the sacred space. Off they would go to the forest to perform secret rites for about two hours; after which, the candidate would be covered again and escorted back to the *kooshay* hut. The candidate is warned not to reveal what happened during these secret night rituals or he and his family would suffer terrible consequences. Believing this, the secret rituals are never revealed; other stories are invented to appease curious family members and insistent friends. Yet we do know that everything that was done during those secret night rites was to prepare the candidate to receive the "magickal power" from spirit, the powers of the deities and the ancestors.

Since the candidate could not bathe or change his clothing, he would be allowed to sleep as long as he wanted because the spirit was working within the candidate's head and should not be disturbed or interrupted. Keep in mind that if there was more than one candidate, the same *kooshay* space would be shared in silence. Usually, five would be the most at any given time, others would have to wait until the next available time. Also, the space was necessary for the apprentices to go through the initiatory process of their next level. So the medicine man was kept quite busy with the woes of the village as well as the initiation of candidates. No wonder that he had such power over the villagers who both feared and respected him. This too is one of the main reasons that initiation would be only at certain times of the year. Time was needed to collect berries, seeds, leaves, barks, shells, feathers, bird eggs, animals, and animal parts. Time was needed to prepare poultices, herbal remedies, herbal teas and other healing concoctions. Only the medicine man and his apprentices could collect the ingredients in certain months during various phases of the sun and the moon, as well as particular seasons. Exactness and preciseness is the main skill of all of the medicine men and women who practice "magick".

Every other evening of the candidate's incarceration, a ceremony would be held outside of the *kooshay* hut by the medicine man, the apprentices, and the drummers. Sometimes the family would be invited to participate in the ceremony, and other times, no one would be invited. At no time would the candidate be allowed to attend or even be seen. All the candidate could do was to lay quiet and listen.

If by chance the candidate would scream out or yell audibly for any reason, they would be instantly beaten by the medicine man for disobeying. If it happened again, then the candidate would be dismissed with a threat worse than death if he revealed any secret that he had learned up to the time of his dismissal. Strict obedience was required to the medicine man in order to stay in his good graces.

Each night, the medicine man would wash the head of the candidate and replace the food, except the bird eggs and the cloth head wrap, all of which are being done in secret. The night before the final festivities was the preparation of the "soul vessel." Fingernail clippings, toenail clippings, locks of hair from the head, underarms, pubic hair, and spittle were placed in a hollow gourd and sealed with strips of vines. The medicine man would then take the sealed gourd to a secret shrine that was well hidden. The candidate was told that the ancestors would always know wherever he was in the world at all times and they would be able to protect him from all evil things. It would be many years later before the medicine man would reveal the whereabouts of the sacred shrine of soul vessels.

No food or drink would be given to the candidate twenty-four hours prior to the final ceremony. Songs and dance movements had to be perfect for the coming-out ceremony. New clothes had to be readied, feast foods had to be prepared, relatives and friends had to come from afar to participate in the festivities of the initiation.

At high noon of the last day, the drumming would start when given the signal to do so by the medicine man. The villagers would begin to gather to start the necessary songs and prayers to every ancestor and every deity. Without stopping the momentum, people would ease away and return, but not all at once. Drummers would play in shifts because the drums must never cease. They must flow into each dance movement as well as each song—no pauses, no breaks, no rests. Otherwise the spirits will think that this was not worthy of them. They would think that no one sang their praises enough. They would think these people were lazy and insulting; therefore, they wouldn't come.

But, the louder the drums became, the more frenzied the singing became. At this time, every invited guest would be in place and would not dare to leave for any reason. About nine hours after starting, the apprentices would be in place to escort the shrouded candidates to the center of the now formed circle. Fire bowls would have been placed in strategic spots to lend some light to the festivities. Once the candidates would be lined up, then visiting chiefs and rulers from nearby villages would come forth to offer prayers and gifts to the ancestors and the deities. Meanwhile, the candidates are very hungry and extremely tired but cannot speak even when they begin to feel faint and lightheaded and confused; which was a true sign that the spirit was about to take possession. The deity would always enter the magician's body by way of the back of the head, causing him to speak, act, and think exactly as the deity. The deity would then be able to lend the magician some magickal powers to control the wind and the rain; to control fertility in man, woman, animals and earth's growing things; to heal disease, ailments, pain, injuries; the power to protect the villagers during war; to protect the warriors as they fought; as well as to communicate directly to the deities and ancestors. Only the "highly initiated" could perform this type of "magick." The celebration is led by the medicine man as he is saluted by the village for his successes. During this celebration which is always a part of the initiation rites, the medicine man is showered with gifts, such as lambs, chickens, fabrics, rare feathers, animal skins, animal heads, all kinds of eggs, and even "money," if it exists.

The candidates, having passed through the second level of initiation, work with the medicine man for the next two to three years; thereby, becoming his apprentice. To become a man or woman of magick requires a long process of learning how to identify all plants, herbs, berries, bushes, trees, tree leaves, rocks, soil, twigs, animals, and animal parts. No words of power are taught until after the fifth-year initiation ceremony which lasts for thirty-three days in *kooshay*. Only then are words of power given to activate the magical properties of all natural things. These proper chants, words, and songs are taught to the candidate in complete secrecy and stringent vows of obedience to the ancestors, deities, and the teacher.

During this level of initiation, the candidates are taken in the very late hours of night to the river or stream or to a secret space in the forest that has been deemed sacred. The hunter warriors line up on one side of the river, and the candidate is thrown into the river while blindfolded. As the candidate swims for some kind of safety, the warriors are throwing faux spears into the river; the candidate does not know the spears are fake or even which way to swim to safety. Here is where he must manifest his adeptness for survival. Immediately, he feels the motion of the tide to sense the direction that he must swim to safety. Once he reaches the banks of the river, still blindfolded, he is escorted by a warrior to the fire circle. In the meantime, the next candidate is thrown into the river to experience the same ordeal. When all of the candidates have been seated, some of whom are bleeding and bruised, they are then hustled to a trot around the fire circle. No drums are beaten at this phase of the initiation, only chants which become faster and faster as they run faster and faster. The warriors stand close together in a circle while keeping the candidate on the run in and out of the fire until the medicine man calls a halt. The candidate is shoved to the bare ground by the warrior, where he will stay put for the rest of the night. Just before the sun rises, the warriors escort the candidates, who are wearied, bruised, burned, cut, and a little frightened, back to their *kooshay* hut where their wounds and burns are tended to by advanced apprentices. The candidates are now allowed to eat the food that has been prepared by their family; after which, they sleep. For the next three days, the candidates recover in silence and seclusion. Then the medicine man selects a candidate to be drilled for one hour with no breaks about all of the ancestral chants as well as all of the spirit characteristics and titles and the names of the ancestors of the tribe. Storytelling about the history of the village and its warriors, victories, defeats, and traditions are all part of the curriculum of this level of initiation.

On the twenty-first night of the initiation, the deities of the tribe are infused with the candidate by way of scarification. The outside area of each shoulder, each knee, and each ankle is meticulously carved a symbol that identifies the entity that has already chosen the candidate. These symbols are carved with a ceremonial knife and/or ceremonial stone that is sharp as a razor. Each candidate receives a symbol different from anyone else's, yet each symbol is a powerful magickal necessity. Each symbol has a magickal name that will be used during particular magickal operations. No one else may use those symbols or names unless fully initiated into the magickal traditions of the tribe.

At sunrise of the last day of *kooshay*, all of the candidates are escorted to the banks of the river to be bathed and blessed. Blessing the candidate takes on the form of full-body painting with a white chalky substance mixed with water. The apprentices work many hours to perfect the design of the spirit symbols. Every part of the body, except the genital area, must receive a painted symbol. Inspection by the medicine man is intense and timely, making sure that any mistake or error in placement, size, and accuracy is corrected before the main ceremony begins at dusk.

Each candidate is aware that they must have an additional initiation ritual within a year of the present neophyte initiation to "marry" the spirit that chooses them, be it male or female. They know that a separate hut must be built as a shrine for that spirit wife or spirit husband. It must contain all of the tools, banners, colors, fabrics, fruits, nuts, berries, foods, and animal parts that are representative of that entity. They know that at least one or two nights a week must be spent alone with that "wife or husband" for the rest of their life, regardless of where they might live in the world. These shrines must be maintained only by the candidate himself. And no one else is allowed to enter that shrine unless he is a high initiate, and even then, that visit must be for a very short time.

As the time for the great ritual of initiation nears, the entire village is excited and nervous because every detail of the preparations must be exact and precise according to the instructions of the medicine man. No matter how many times that such a ritual is experienced, each one feels as though it is the first one.

Dusk has arrived, and the drumming begins. The villagers are dressed in their finery, the elders take their place, the medicine man makes his grand entrance with his rattle made of snake bones in one hand and the tail of a lion or elephant or of some great beast killed by a hunter/warrior. The medicine man wears charms around his neck, his upper arms, his wrists, his waist, his thighs, his knees, his ankles and sometimes the calves of his legs. He is completely costumed in his head piece, animal skins, and painted symbols that denote his status.

The apprentices start the sacred fire in the center of the village compound, while the elders are seated in the space where the sun rises. The hierarchy of dignitaries starts the ceremonial circle around the sacred fire. Women and children, unless initiated into the hierarchy, must remain outside of the circle. The songs are started by the elders with the accompaniment of the drums and all of the villagers. Then songs tell the history of the ancestors and their great deeds and how much they mean to everyone present. After about two hours of such praise and adoration of the ancestors, the medicine man gives the signal to an apprentice to dance the candidates into the circle. With the appearance of the candidtates, the villagers vigorously release the screams, whistles, yells and chants. As each candidate enters the circle, he salutes the medicine man, bending on one knee, to receive the dubbing of the animal tail and the snake-bone rattle. Also, at this time, the first talismanic charm is placed around the neck of the candidate. The candidate dances to the elders with the same salute and receives their blessings. The dancing and singing become louder and stronger, and the candidates let loose all of their pent-up emotions and happiness that this ordeal is finally over after thirty-three days of seclusion and silence and agony.

The ceremony introduces each candidate to the deities. It is at this time that the spirit chooses the "head" it wants to reside in. When the medicine man announces the adoption, the elders agree and the villagers cheer and the song apropos to that deity is sung. Each candidate receives his sprit, and the celebration continues throughout the night with breaks for feasting and socializing. As the sun rises, the candidates must return to the *kooshay* hut to gather their belongings and to receive final instructions from the medicine man. Responsibilities of service to the medicine man are outlined before they, the candidates, are dismissed to their families and homes. The apprentices clean the ceremonial areas, and then they are allowed to return to their respective homes to rest.

The candidates who are now called *tibon* or "little magicians" are allowed three days to be with family and friends before moving back into the compound of the medicine man. Usually, after three to five more years of study under the medicine man, the tibon is sent to live in the tribal village that is in need of a medicine man. This stay could be short-lived if the tibon does not have success in his magickal operations. It is not unheard of for a tibon to be returned to his village of initiation for more seasoning when he fails to manifest the proper results. Of course, it is embarrassing for the medicine man, the elders, the family, and the entire village. Usually, for the tibon, it's back to square one if he still wants to be a medicine man and the ancestors still want him to be one. Interest and enthusiasm is not enough to be a good medicine man; it takes intelligence, patience, and, above all, focus. The medicine man will always remind the tibon that magic is not a game or child's play; it is serious and dangerous work—hard work.

The candidates must now prepare for the most terrifying ordeal of magick, and it doesn't help to have been told of the experiences of others. They begin a trek into the forests for ten days without food or drink; they must survive on what the forest presents to them. On this journey, they are not allowed to kill anything for consumption. In future, more lengthy treks and certain kills are allowed for eating and for collecting ingredients necessary for magical work.

There is one full gourd of an herbal mixture which they must drink a small amount of three times a day. The medicine man prepares this drink for each candidate to be able to talk to the ancestors who are waiting for him in the forest. Every seventh tree the candidate finds will be his sleeping quarters. When he finds his first tree in which to sleep, he must exorcise the surrounding area of the tree and then ask the tree for permission to sleep with the ancestors in the branches. The herbal drink is poured in libation to the four directions—north, south, east, and west, after which, the candidate takes three gulps. Within twenty minutes, he will start to have dizziness and weakness. He knows that some part of him must stay alert and on guard because of the terrible dangers that surround him day and night. He also knows that this is the time for praying to the ancestors for protection. The drink forces him to surrender his will, and the candidate enters into the dream time. He senses that it is time for the second drink, and he takes three more gulps. This time, he goes deeper into the world of dream time. He will remember everything he experienced on this journey. Because he faced all of his fears and doubts, he knows he is a better man. He now believes he is a true magician, and now, he faces the rest of his journey as well as future journeys with courage and excitement. It has been said that some candidates have returned to the village with white hair or face changes or something else has been changed, but they never return the same. Some candidates have never returned or have been seen remaining in the forest for the rest of their lives or have gone to a mountain top or cave to live with the ancestors, so they say. It is truly a magickal journey.

Chapter 8

Preface

Blood is more than a life force; it is a message from our ancestors, what today is called DNA.

Blood has a strange effect on anybody and anything. The smell of blood attracts animals such as sharks, dogs, and wild animals. The taste of blood is peculiar in itself. However strange the taste, there are Europeans who make blood pudding for meals. There are also Masai who drink the blood of their cattle for nourishment. I do know that certain occult groups use blood as a magickal tool. Blood is also a symbolic tool in a Christian communion ritual.

Just the sight of blood would make me gag because, as a child, I associated blood with pain and death. The idea of me being stuck with a needle would send me to pray to God to say that I was so sorry for whatever I did that was so bad to deserve a needle in the arm or the behind. And they were no small needles like what they have today. We used to call them horse needles because they were so long and so big and they hurt.

As a youngster, I had three girlfriends who decided we should have a secret club. None of us knew what a secret club was or exactly what they did. But we knew that to join the club, we had to draw blood from each other's fingers to become blood sisters. On the day we were to have the beginning of our secret club, nobody showed up. It would be many years later before I would know just how important that binding would be now, or just how dangerous the mixing of blood is, with people that are no longer in my life.

The Blood Rituals for Initiation

Blood rituals are an absolute necessity for any level of initiation into the magickal mysteries, so thought the tribesman of Africa. The blood carries the life force, courage, strength, wisdom, and creativeness of the ancestors. Even though many traditions in ancient times have practiced human sacrifice in ceremonies, and not just African traditions, animal sacrifices were just as important and necessary for their ritual practices. Animals are chosen based on the characteristics of the deity as well as the level of the ceremony itself. Chickens, lambs, bulls, monkeys, and goats are usually sacrificed for religious ceremonies. Each animal is likened to a great deity as well as to the ancestors, new and old.

The three necessary ingredients for a magical ceremony are as follows:

- Sound—drumming, singing, tongue clicking, chanting, whistling, mantras
- Movement—dancing, leaping, jumping, clapping hands, stomping feet
- Leadership—a magick man who has the knowledge of the ritual and the power that is necessary to invoke the gods and the ancestors

Blood rituals for initiation serve many purposes. An initiate may need to be cleansed of any negative or demonic energies to strengthen the link between the ancestors and the initiate or to build the magickal power of the initiate and "open" his head to receive the communications from spirit and the ancestors. Blood rituals are used to remove diseases, bond tribes, bring good weather and bountiful harvest, or ensure fertility for the village. Regardless of the recipient of the blood sacrifice, they are always officiated by the medicine man. These sacred rituals are expensive and must be carried out properly for the magick to work.

The animal to be sacrificed must be chosen with care by the medicine man. The animal, if a goat, lamb, ram or bull, is washed thoroughly, fed, and then decorated with vines, leaves, flowers, or shells. Magickal words are shouted for the animal, songs are sung, and sincere thanks are spoken to the animal. It is at this point of the preparation that the medicine man escorts the animal, with the help of apprentices, to a shrine deep in the forest. It is at the shrine that the animal is introduced to the ancestors for their approval. Libations are poured in all four directions. The animal is then escorted back to the village amidst singing, drumming, and dancing. If the animal that is to be sacrificed is a bull—the highest form of the blood ritual—it must be wrestled to the ground. With a finely honed knife or a smoothly sharpened stone, the throat of the bull is quickly and expertly cut. The first blood is immediately smeared on the medicine man, who then bends down to drink the blood. The animal is then hoisted upside down to drain the blood freely into gourd containers. The blood is quickly smeared from head to toe over each candidate, who then drink some before it coagulates. Any blood left over will be used at a later time for healing operations. Even though the elders and the rest of the village will watch the entire process, they are not allowed to receive this blood at this time because this is part of the initiation for magickal work.

The ritual continues with the sacrifice of the bull and then preparing it for cooking. The village is festive with dancing, singing, and drumming. Cooking fires are set up in each direction, where the meat is cooked by the men. The other fires are used by women to cook vegetables and herbal drinks. The initiates gather around the fire in the west to start their chanting of thanksgiving to the ancestors and deities. By this time, the blood smeared on their bodies has dried;

and the quick small steps circling the fire are started. All eyes are staring into the fire as spears are handed to each initiate, including the medicine man. The villagers gather to watch the proceedings, but this time, they do not sing or dance, as the entrance of the deities is about to happen. The initiates thrust the spear tips into the fire and then quickly remove them while calling out the name of the requested deity. Soon, one or two of the initiates lets out a howl or scream and falls backwards and begins to swirl and run in circles all over the compound. Others begin to be "possessed" with similar howls and screams. The villagers by now have formed a large circle around the open area of the compound. Only the cooks are left out of the circle. As each initiate whirls to a person in the circle, that person is "blessed" by the deity with the touching of the spear to a certain part of the body. That person drops out of the circle. When everyone has been blessed, they bring gifts to the initiate that has blessed them. The "possessed" ones return to their fire circle while the villagers begin to sing. As soon as the deity departs, the initiate runs through the forest to the river or to a shrine in the forest to wash off the blood and returns to the village for feasting and celebration. This particular ritual may be done once or twice a year to enhance the initiates with magickal powers.

When a person believes they've been cursed, they take a black or white chicken to the medicine man for a special ritual to offset that curse. The chicken is blessed by the medicine man who then requires the offended one to hold the chicken and plead for the release of the curse. He asks the chicken to absorb the curse. The medicine man literally bites off the tongue of the chicken and wraps it in a piece of animal skin and then burns the chicken tongue to ashes, thereby releasing the spell. Taking the chicken by the neck, the medicine man deftly cuts the throat of the chicken. And the blood pours into the hands of the client who then marks his forehead, his cheeks, and his chin with blood. The medicine man immediately cuts off the head of the chicken and drains the rest of the blood into a gourd. He raises the chicken over the head of the client while saying specific incantations. He then instructs the client to cook the chicken thoroughly and eat it with his family. The reason behind this action is that the chicken took on the curse and released it to the undergods and, in doing so, received blessings for his being sacrificed. Once the family eats the sacrifice, they too are blessed. In exchange for the ritual, the family must give the medicine man something of value, such as feathers from a rare and/or sacred bird, a live animal, baskets, cloth made by hand, or even money, if it was available. Nevertheless, a fair exchange must always be made for magickal work that is completed, whether it works or not.

When an individual has a disease or an illness, the medicine man may require a larger sacrifice to be used. Usually a lamb or goat is sacrificed in order to determine the type of illness and its origin. The entrails from a sacrificed animal tell this story, and the medicine man interprets the position of the entrails. A sacrificial animal must always be cut in the throat and the blood drained into a proper container. After all of the blood has been drained and placed aside, the underside of the animal is slit open to allow the entrails to fall out on the ground. Now, the medicine man interprets the signs and symbols of each organ according to how it is placed on the ground. The medicine man reads the whole story of what the disease is, how long it will last, where the disease came from, who is responsible, and finally, will it be fatal or not. The medicine man sprinkles herbs over the entrails, and according to where and how the herbs fall on the entrails or the ground, a cure will be communicated to the medicine man. The entrails are completely removed from the animal and placed outside of the hut on a huge leaf. There they will dry out and later be used in the formula for healing. The skin of the animal is removed, and the flesh is cooked. Once it is cooked, everything of the animal, including the entrails, are ceremoniously presented to the ancestors. Later, the client and his family and the medicine man will eat the cooked animal after the ancestors have had their fill.

There is a blood ritual that is used for determining a person's guilt or innocence for a crime. Once the accused is brought before the elders and the medicine man, the person who accuses would state the crime, usually stealing cattle or some animal. The medicine man uncovers a rusty knife or razor blade so that everyone can see. This ritual is performed in front of the entire village, and whatever the verdict is, they will support it. The accused watches the medicine man cut his leg, and there is no bleeding; the medicine man chooses one of his apprentices to be cut the same way, and again, there is no bleeding, which means innocence. The accused is brought forth and is cut in the same place as the medicine man and the apprentice and in the same manner with the same tool. If he bleeds, he is guilty, and severe punishment is swiftly carried out. If he does not bleed, then he is innocent and released immediately.

Affairs of the heart are always brought to the medicine man by women and men. If a woman wants to be with a particular man and is having a difficult time in getting his attention or if a woman does not want to lose her husband to another woman, then her menstrual blood is put into food that she must serve only for him to eat. This ritual is done over a specific period of time along with incantations. It has been told that once the woman gets the man this way, he will become repulsive to her and she will never get rid of him.

At the same time, a man who desires a woman must place some of his semen into something that she will eat, and once he gets her, he can never get rid of her.

The lunar ritual of the goddess is performed by the medicine woman and her apprentices. Once the menstrual period begins, the young woman goes into the forest to a secret shrine. Her menstrual blood is collected in a gourd each day. The gourd contains herbs, bark, stones, river water, leaves, bird feathers, and a few secret ingredients. When the gourd has a certain amount of the blood, the woman then sits in a cross-legged position to allow the blood to seep into the earth. After about an hour, she then must sit upon a rock or a large stone. Each night, she burns the contents of the gourd. Once the blood has "cooked," she takes that gourd to the river or brook to empty the contents as well as to clean the gourd to be used the next month. After cleaning the gourd, the woman wraps the gourd in leaves and/or cloth or skins and returns it to the altar that honors the goddess. When her period is finished, she bathes thoroughly before returning to the village.

A woman's menstrual cycle is considered a sacred and private time between the goddess and the woman. It is believed that the menstrual blood is sacred because it contains the necessary ingredients to sustain the life of a new human being for nine months. It is the very best of that woman. Never is it considered waste or negative or evil. The menstrual cycle is an acknowledgment of all of her female ancestors that represent the bloodline and prepares her to eventually join the ancestors. When a woman's menstrual flow begins, she must not participate in any type of ritual that includes men, lest she be contaminated with evil demons and bad spirits. It was the female ancestors who chose to be separate and apart from community and others during her cleansing time. Women who are infertile will go to the sacred shrine of the goddesses to place their hands on a rock or stone that belongs to a virgin's blood, with permission, of course. The woman then must give an offering to the shrine as well as the young girl.

A child who is ill may require the menstrual blood of his or her mother in order to be cured. The medicine woman has a method that makes this blood magickal and powerful enough to cure. Once the blood is mixed with herbs and water, the sick child is fed the potion

The burial ritual is a blood ritual with a twist. Once a person was dead, the corpse would be taken to a grove that had sharpened spearheads located in strategic spots. The body was laid on top of these spearheads which would pierce the body and allow the blood to flow freely in the earth. To have a single drop of the blood of the dead touch you would be taboo according to the law.

At least once a year during a high holy season, the elders sponsor a community cleansing ritual. All members of the village attend, whether near or far. The festival ritual would last at least one week, and it involves everyone in the village. Sometimes two or three villages will join together. The animals to be sacrificed for the ancestors are chosen with great care long before the date of the ritual. Everyday, the animals are washed and brushed and well fed. The sacrificial animals could be chickens, rams, bulls, lambs, goats, birds, monkeys, and sometimes snakes, and they are kept separate and apart from other animals. Every day, the apprentices walk or tend the animals. They also sing certain songs, chants, and prayers to the animals. The elders form their circle around the pen of the animals to encourage them to be brave as well as honored for the contribution of their lives. Each night, the animals are praised and blessed and sung to by the villagers. Each person is allowed to gently touch the animal to remember them to the ancestors. The animals seem to enjoy this special time because they are very calm and they seem to understand what is about to happen.

When the time is right, villagers and guests form a large circle around a huge fire that has been made in the center of the compound. Song after song; dance after dance; chant after chant is kept going for hours. Families are reunited, old acquaintances are renewed, and the guests are introduced to the elders. Each night, three animals are chosen by the elder to be sacrificed. The blood is collected in gourds, and each person kneels before the elder to receive a splash of blood on the face. Some people receive symbols drawn on the face, arms, and legs with the blood. Meanwhile, the songs are still going strong, along with the frenzied drumbeating. Adults and children alike are dressed for the occasion as they offer gifts to the elders and the ancestors. Each family has a separate shrine for their ancestors, and each ancestor's name is memorized by each family member. Special foods and drinks are prepared for the ancestors even though they are fed everyday. But at this sacred time, all of the ancestors return to the village to receive the gifts, the adoration, as well as to hear the requests, desires, and the problems. Once the animals have been properly cooked, the ancestors are fed first. Next are the elders and the medicine man, and then the villagers and guests. Everyone keeps the blood blessing on them for days or until the blood dries and peels away. There is very little sleep to be had during this time, except for the children, who try to stay awake.

Bones from the sacrificed animals are kept by the elders and medicine men, but a small bone is given to each family. The tail, ears, and eyes are always given to the medicine man. The entrails that are edible are prepared separately for the elders, and those parts that are not cooked are presented to the medicine man for his cure medicines. The tongue of the animal is presented to the family that donated the sacrificed animal, even if the animal was stolen in a cattle raid. The tongue of the animal represents how the ancestors are able to communicate with the family members. It is then prepared for their meal. There is no part of the animal that is not used or eaten; not a drop of blood is lost, nor a drop of fat wasted. This animal is revered by every person in the celebration.

Blood rituals that unite villages are commonly held in order to protect each other from other tribal attacks, such as kidnapping of children and young girls, cattle rustling, and, of course, war. The ritual is arranged by the elders of both villages who decide the place, time, and day of the ritual. This is a major ritual that must be approved by the ancestors of both villages. When the details have been agreed upon, the preparations are started. When everyone from both villages meet, the festivities begin by "calling in" the ancestors with drumming, singing, and dancing. Both village elders sit in a circle in the center of the compound drinking fermented beer. The medicine man greets the visiting medicine man with magickal words of welcome and gestures of goodwill. The visiting medicine man responds with magickal words and gestures of thankfulness. All of the people form a huge circle around the medicine men and the elders. Only when both medicine men are satisfied that all of the ancestors have arrived and approved the continuation of the ritual do the medicine men approach the elders. Using fetishes made from a tail of a wild animal, the medicine men brandish each other from head to toe in order to drive away any demon spirit that might have slipped into the ritual. Then the elders receive the "cleansing"; after which, the village people are blessed. The medicine men retreat to the forest shrine while the villagers take a break and socialize.

After about two hours in the forest, the two medicine men return to the village compound in all of their regalia. Their bodies are completely covered with paint made from berries and plants; they are adorned with feathers, shells, and plant leaves. Having drunk their own powerful potions, they both are reeling to the drumming which had just begun. Everybody returns to the circle full of expectations and excitement. The medicine men approach the elders with great humility and honor, asking permission to continue the ritual. Permission is granted, and the medicine men reveal their knives or sharpened stones with wild and grand gestures. Soon, both of them collapse to the ground. Everyone becomes instantly quiet, drums stop beating, singing ceases, even the children and babies remain quiet. Everything stops moving. Everything is quiet and still. All eyes are on the medicine men lying on the ground in front of all the elders. In a few minutes, even though it seems longer, the medicine men begin to roll over and over on the ground, uttering unknown words and strange sounds. The ancestors have arrived. Still, everyone remains quiet. The oldest elder of each village stands to acknowledge the entrance of the ancestors by speaking out similar words and sounds. Each elder then takes a turn to stand and repeat the action of welcome. Meanwhile, the medicine men are still rolling and rolling. After the last elder has finished his salute, the village people and guests sing a song of praise and adoration to the ancestors; no drums are allowed to sound at this time.

It is at this time that the apprentices from both villages make their entrance, bearing gifts and sacrificial offerings. Chickens are first to be offered as a sacrifice. Each elder should have at least one chicken, but if the villages are very poor, then only two chickens are sacrificed. The wealthier the village, the more elaborate the ritual. The medicine men stop rolling but continue the speaking of words and sounds. They take the chicken from the elder and immediately chop the head of the chicken off. The medicine men start to twirl about and around as they hold the bleeding chicken by the legs. Blood is splattered everywhere and on everyone. Everyone tries to position themselves to receive the blood blessing. Of course, the elders are on the first line to receive "the gift of life" from the ancestors.

Again, the medicine men collapse to the ground. An apprentice brings the herbal potion that they have been drinking since long before the ceremony started. This herbal potion puts the medicine men in such a psychic state of mind that will allow the spirits of the ancestors to speak through the medicine men. Drinking the herbal potion causes the medicine men to sit up straight and call for the second sacrifice, which is usually a goat or lamb. The chickens have been removed to another part of the compound to be prepared for the coming feast. The goat is blessed with different kinds of herbs and rain or river water; he is saluted for his courage to be sacrificed for the ancestors. The medicine men lift the goat high above their heads and walk slowly around the circle while singing songs of obedience to the ancestors. The walk to the elders is performed even slower, which acknowledges their long life. Reaching the place of the elders, the goat's throat is expertly cut so that the blood drains quickly. This time, the apprentices are there to catch the blood in special clay pots that have been prepared just for this occasion by both villages. The villagers start to sing, but still, the drums are not to be played. The medicine men again salute the elders while in the trance state by dipping each finger into the gourd of blood. When all of the fingers have been so blessed, the elders lift their hands high so that everyone can see the initiation of welcome from the ancestors. The villagers line up to receive the blood prints from the elders; each person kneels in front of a visiting elder who marks their face with ten fingerprints. Now the drums begin to beat slowly and softly, the chanting joins in with the drumbeat. After everyone has been blessed, the elders retire to a hut to eat with the medicine men and retire for the night. Day two will bring more blood rituals and sacrifices. Day three is the last day of the blood initiation; therefore, it is the most important step in the process.

This part of the ceremony is performed at night in conjunction with the full moon. The medicine men lead the elders into the center of the circle formed by the villagers. There is no drumming nor singing at this time. Once the elders have been seated in a straight line that faces east, the medicine men instruct everyone to be quiet and still. The ancestors are invoked to please pay attention to the proceedings. The apprentices start the central fire; the medicine men begin their chant and dance around the fire. There is now the drinking of the herbal potion by the elders and the medicine men. Prayer after prayer is spoken by each elder, and everyone must listen closely. After the final elder is finished praying, the medicine men bring a carved stone bowl to the eldest of the elders from each village. The visiting medicine man makes a small cut on the middle finger of the left hand of the elder; seven drops of blood is let into the small stone bowl. Once the two elders have been initiated, the remaining elders receive the same type of cut to mix their blood. Finally, the medicine men cut each other's finger to add blood to the bowl. The blood is mixed thoroughly, and each elder is marked on the forehead with the mixed blood. All of the children from both villages are brought by their parents and marked on the chest with the mixed blood.

The medicine men and the elders drink more of the herbal potion. The drums are given the signal to start. The medicine men bring in the bull that is to be sacrificed. The bull has been washed clean and adorned with flowers and vines. The bull is presented to the ancestors as a gift of thanks for the approval of the uniting of the two villages which now become one united front. The bull's throat is cut in such a way as to make the spurting blood easier to handle. All of the apprentices are there to assist the medicine man with the sacrifice. When the animal is dead, the tail is cut off and presented to the eldest of the elders. Usually, there are two bulls sacrificed; one representing each village. The medicine men will receive the skins and the teeth of the bulls. Every other edible part of the bull is cooked to be served for the feast. The medicine men will add honey and cow's milk to the bull's blood, and everyone comes forward for one gulp. If any is left over, the medicine men must finish the blood mixture.

Now, the festivities start and will last for three days. And on the seventh day, everyone will go to their respective homes. The people from both villages have been properly united by blood and can now be married to each other, live in each other's village, trade with each other, as well as to go to war as one unit.

When the festival is over, the compound is thoroughly cleansed physically and mystically, dismissing the ancestors and their guests. Then everyone rests and gossips.

Chapter 9

Preface

One balmy Sunday afternoon, my grandfather took me to see his girlfriend, Ms. Bert. I always liked Ms. Bert because she talked to me, and not at me. About a week after the visit, I was told to take a bath (and it wasn't even Saturday night yet) and put on my Sunday clothes. I already knew not to ask any type of question about where I am going or what everybody is so sad about. After dressing in my Sunday best, we walked to our neighborhood church, and I was told to sit by my grandfather. He was the most handsome man in the world, and I loved looking at his face. I never tired of staring, wondering how he talked, or how he ate with only one tooth in the front of his mouth. My grandfather fascinated me because he had so many girlfriends, and they were all nice to me.

Sitting in the front pew with my grandfather and all dressed up in my Sunday best was a very happy time. Because I was smiling, my grandfather scowled at me, and I started to pout. As I looked around the church, more people were coming in, people that I knew never came to church. I was told to turn around and be still. People were dressed in black, and some brought beautiful flowers to stand next to this shiny wooden box. There were so many flowers that they had to put them on the side aisle where I was sitting. They were carnations, all colors, smelling to high heaven. The men dressed in black stood in front of this shiny box and lifted the lid back, and they started to fix the dress of somebody. All I could think of was, What is going on? What is happening? Why am I here? When the people in black moved away, people started to scream, holler, cry, and even faint. The church nurses would run to attend them. I started to panic and cry too. I just didn't know why. I turned to my grandfather who sat tall and very stiff, very quiet. I turned my eyes to the shiny box, and lo and behold! There was a woman sleeping, and she looked like Ms. Bert. It didn't take long for me to know that it was Ms. Bert. I sat quietly while the preacher ranted and raved. The choir sang. And everybody cried except me and my grandfather.

The men in black came back to the shiny box and covered Ms. Bert with a white satin blanket. And then the strangest thing happened; they gave my grandfather a white satin handkerchief. He stood up and took my hand to walk with him to the shiny box. Now, I was really scared, so scared that I started to cry, and it seemed that it was a signal for everybody in the church to scream, cry out, and, of course, pass out. By this time, I was totally numb with fear. The lid to the shiny box was closed, and the men in black, plus some of the other men in the church carried the box outside to a long black car. My grandfather and I, along with four other people, squeezed into the following car. Soon, there was a long line of cars with a sticker on the windshield that spelled F-U-N-E-R-A-L. The ride was slow and long. When we arrived at the cemetery, Ms. Bert was lowered into the ground. Everybody threw flowers and dirt on top of the shiny box with Ms. Bert. I thought of what she was going to do when she woke up. I cried harder.

Fortunately, there are many tools to bring awareness of death to children and to adults who have intensive fears about death. It wasn't until I was initiated that I really understood the process of death. So I can sympathize with anyone who is afraid of dying and what could possibly await them—the hell that the Christians say is the punishment, and the heaven that will be the reward. No wonder we fear death, no wonder we mourn and grieve, no wonder everybody wants to go to heaven, but nobody wants to die.

The Death Rites of Passage

Death is answering to the call of the ancestors to join them now. Very little sadness or grieving is experienced at this time because eventually everyone will become an ancestor. Death is to be celebrated, and birth is to be grieved.

The traditional religions of the world always keep a sacred space for those who have passed on, thus becoming our ancestors. The strong belief is that the ancestor will always protect the family from harm and evil. However, the promise is also to honor the ancestor with the items that they loved when they were alive. Some items may be certain foods, sweets, jewelry, clothes, or even music. Worshipping the deities blends with the rituals for the ancestors. Shrines are erected within the home or a special place outside of the home, and they are scrupulously cared for—being cleaned and replacing foodstuffs regularly. The Ancestor must never be forgotten, because without them, you would not be where you are today; this is the belief of all villagers. Petitioning an ancestor for assistance is practiced on a consistent basis—giving gifts regularly to the ancestor such as flowers, food, incense (burning certain crushed leaves and berries that produce sweet aromas), and any other items that the ancestor favors.

Because ancestor worship is so intense, the African religion began to unfold with the African gods and goddesses at par with the ancestors. The belief is simplistic in that the ancestors became the messengers and the go-between to the deities.

When a member of the family dies, certain rituals must be followed, otherwise the dead one will be unable to find the ancestors and he will stay lost forever. There are specific rituals for children who have died, for the elders, and most certainly for the medicine man. It has been told that a medicine man will be told by the ancestors the exact day and time of his death. Therefore, the medicine man has time to arrange his affairs so that there is no confusion with his legacy. The medicine man knows that he must pass all of the secret knowledge to someone who has been proven worthy, man or woman. The medicine man cannot die until he has passed his knowledge to someone who will carry on the magical tradition of the ancestors. If he dies without passing the knowledge, then he will not be welcomed into the realm of the ancestors and will remain a lost soul that roams the nether world.

When an adult dies, his or her body is washed completely with a mixture of herbs and water. The deceased will be dressed in the best way possible in order to meet with the ancestors proudly. The hut is made ready to receive, first, the elders, the medicine man, and then the villagers. The deceased is placed in a chair or at least in a sitting erect position, and the stools or mats are arranged in front of him. The elders will enter the hut to sing and chant, which will guide the deceased to the ancestors. The elders will seat themselves in front of the dead body and begin to talk to it. Sincere requests are made to the deceased one to carry back to the ancestors. Problems in the village are discussed aloud, as well as news from afar and gossip from other villages. This activity continues for three days and three nights. Never is the body left unattended, and a family member is always present to receive the guests that come to give messages to the ancestors.

While the deceased is still in the hut, the medicine man will remove some part of the dead body in order for the family to set up an ancestral shrine. This removal can only take place after the third day. There are some tribes that require the widow to wear an appendage of her husband as a necklace. However, the medicine man usually treats the appendage with herbal potions that dry it quickly. The deceased may have given instructions before death as to what part of his body is to remain unburied—a tooth, finger, or toe. Even an ear may be kept to be worn around the neck or the waist. The family shrine will also receive a remnant of the deceased. This remnant is usually hair, nails, or teeth. There must be special containers made by hand that will contain some special essence of the ancestor. Of course, it takes the specific magical powers of the medicine man to invite that family ancestor to be housed in the handmade urn or clay pot. When the ancestor takes up residence in the pot, the family can speak to it at any time. This urn will be passed down to generation after generation. All of the pertinent history and care information will be told over and over again. If the ancestor is not properly maintained, then the family will experience all kinds of havoc, such as infertility, poor harvests, and/or major illnesses. The ancestor must always be appeased.

On the fourth day at dawn, the medicine man accompanies the family to a chosen spot for burial. The medicine man pours a potion of herbs and water, plus other sundry things over the selected spot. Symbols are painted on the ground; after which, berries from a sacred bush are strewn on top of the painted symbols. The family members are given a signal by the medicine man to start stomping over the berries and symbols in order to ward off any demon or unwanted spirits that may be in that chosen spot. Singing and lamenting accompany the stomping which continues until all of the berries are crushed and the painted symbols are erased. Now the men will dig a deep hole just big enough for the body to be placed in a sitting position facing the east. Some favorite possessions of the deceased are placed in the grave, and sometimes, gifts for the ancestors are included, which could be a sweet cake or shells or feathers or anything that the ancestor would really appreciate. Finally, the villagers come to pay their last respects amidst the singing and wailing. As the grave is covered, the stomping on the ground is resumed in order to frighten away any lurking spirit. After the grave has been completely covered, the family members stomp over the grave until it is flat and even with the rest of the ground. Each member of the village places a small stone at the head of the grave to remind the deceased one to remember him to the ancestors. Sometimes, a stone is carved into a figure or a symbol representing the village or the family and placed on the grave. Thus, a shrine is started and will be maintained by the family as long as possible. There are times when the body will be kept in the hut for at least seven days in order for relatives from other villages or places to come to speak to the deceased as well as to pay respects to the grieving family. They will also bring gifts and food for the occasion to be shared with the ancestors and the family. Oddly enough, drums are not usually beaten at a time of bereavement.

If a child dies, it is believed that the child was taken by the ancestors. Burial must occur three days after death. Messages are given to the child to be taken back to the ancestors. The deity that represents death is given strict orders to escort the child directly to the waiting ancestors. Misfortune must be warded away from the spirit of the child. If the child was old enough to walk and talk, then toys and food are buried with him. If one child of a twin set should die, it is a very bad omen. Therefore, the medicine man prepares a specific ritual for this twin that requires the entire village to participate. The surviving twin is escorted to the place where the elders sit to preside. The child is prompted to speak loudly to the deceased sibling. He makes promises to always honor and make sacrifices in his name on his naming day. The family members bring food, toys, and other gifts for the deceased child. The most important gift is the sacrifice of a chicken, monkey, or goat. The animal is washed clean with herbs and other mixtures that the medicine man has prepared for this occasion. Each villager is expected to bring some type of gift that the child will enjoy, because they know that the death of this child can affect each and every one of them in a bad way. The ceremony begins with the medicine man invoking the ancestors of that child. He sings, chants, dances, and brandishes his rattle over the surviving child's head. The villagers join in the singing and chanting as well as some dancing. Basically, this is more of an oral ritual than a celebration. The welfare of the village is at stake, and the villagers are somewhat frightened of the possibility that this deceased child could cause serious harm to anybody. The dead child feels cheated and is jealous that he could not stay with his twin. But if the family and villagers do not forget him and bring him toys and good food, he won't be angry or upset with them. So think the family, villagers, elders and medicine man. The ritual continues with cajoling, petitions, promises, and songs of praise and honor to the deceased child. For three days and three nights, the child is never left alone, nor does the surviving twin leave his sibling alone at any time. At the end of the third night, the dead twin is wrapped in white fabric and then marched through the village as a final blessing to the villagers. The elders and the medicine man are now waiting at the gravesite or at the entrance of a cave where others are also buried. If the child is placed in the ground, he is placed in a fetal position and covered with soil. Afterwards, stones are placed over the entire grave to keep the spirit from escaping back to the village.

There have been some cases of deliberately destroying one twin child because having multiple births was considered bad luck for the entire village. This type of action is still a mystery as to the reason why. There are some tribes that still follow that belief at the present time.

Illnesses that lead to death were believed to be a deed of black magic or the will of the ancestor who may have been angry with the family for not honoring him. Usually, the medicine man would be called in for a consultation to speak with the ancestors to confirm or deny who or what caused the illness or any bad luck for the family. Indeed, the spirit of the ancestor would "possess" the mind and body of the medicine man in order to speak directly with the family. If the ancestor was not to blame for the illness or death, he would advise the family how to protect themselves as well as how to return the evil deed to the one who sent it. Oddly enough, the ancestor's spirit would also advise the family on how much they should pay the medicine man for his assistance. Once the "possession" was finished, the medicine man would have to be fed a meal and drink. Sometimes the spirit would give instructions for healing the afflicted one, or sometimes it would be too late for any treatment. If the death was caused by black magic, then the family would hire the medicine man to return the curse to its sender. Many times, there would be unjust and untrue accusations made on other families or individuals who were made to suffer. Being banished from the village as sorcerers or witches caused many families to break down. Women were the targets for being connected to black magic, innocent or not; they would be exiled to fend for themselves. Sometimes, these unfortunate women would be stoned to death, and their bodies would be left for the vultures; no funeral rites of any kind would be offered. The banished women would roam the forests barely alive because of the harsh treatment by the villagers.

There have been some women who met by chance and started their own village. However, because they were not hunters, they were always on the brink of starvation. So many of them died alone of a broken heart and broken spirit, torn away from their children, husband, family, and friends because one person accused her of black magic. Some husbands have been known to start the rumors that would eventually destroy their wives, especially if they wanted to divorce them but had no just reasons that would satisfy the elders. A few women committed suicide by eating poison roots or berries or leaves, knowing that they would never be able to join the ranks of the ancestors. Others would endure the severe hardship and would look forward to being with the ancestors, especially if they were falsely accused. It would be her revenge against those who banished her from her village life of family and tradition and all that she held sacred.

If a woman's husband dies or is killed, she must endure a ritual of widowhood. This particular ritual varies with each tribe as well as each village. One tribe in particular requires the woman to cut off her dead husband's hand and wear it around her neck as a necklace until such time as the elders will dictate. This act symbolizes the control of the man over his wife, whether he is dead or alive. Another tribe requires the widow to cut off the ears of her dead husband in order for her to always be able to hear her husband's instructions. Yet if the man's wife dies, all that he is required to do is marry quickly in order that his children will be cared for as well as to keep procreation active. Procreation is the foremost reason for marriage.

Death by suicide was practically unheard of in the deep forests. Death by one's own hand would be considered as an evil act against the gods and the ancestors. Life was too precious, no matter how difficult the life would be. The goal was and always has been to keep the bloodlines preserved.

If a warrior died in battle, then he was glorified for his bravery. He never feared death which, of course, made him a formidable enemy. He believed the ancestors would protect him or receive him; he had been trained just for this moment of glory.

If a person was executed for a serious crime, then his body could not be claimed by the family for a proper burial. There have been occasions where the family of the condemned person would be forced into exile. The elders reasoned that the village no longer wanted that bloodline to be continued with them. Depending on the nature of the crime, the death sentence would be carried out somewhere in the forest. Sometimes the punishment would be swift, and other times, it would be long and painful—absolute torture.

If the death was caused by magic, the reaction of the villagers would be to avoid the family and the burial rite. Fearing that the curse would attach itself to someone else was enough for everyone, except the elders, to keep at a distance. Cursing someone to illness and death was real because it had happened too many times before. Everybody believed in it and everybody feared it. Of course, the medicine man became prosperous and important enough to dictate policy to the elders and the villagers. If you did not receive the right protection charms and talismans, then you were vulnerable to any type of magical attack. Every man, woman, and child depended on these magical charms for protection against death by sorcery, and they had to pay the medicine man whatever he asked for, even if the protection didn't last for a long period of time or even if it didn't protect them at all. It was not a matter of choice; it was a matter of survival—anyway you could.

Death is not the final chapter in the ancient African tradition. Death is another initiation. It is a doorway for the soul to transcend into the realm of the ancestors.

Chapter 10

Preface

At the age of fifteen, I decided to take bongo and conga drum lessons at five dollars an hour. It was the first and the last. Trying to hold a drum between my knees was a disaster. Each time I slapped the heads, I would knock the drum to the floor. It was quickly decided that I was definitely not a drummer. Plus, I had poor coordination which resulted in poor rhythm. I was so disappointed that I never touched another drum until I was initiated, and then I had to.

Remembering my past experience, I was too embarrassed to admit I couldn't play. So I tried to fake it. I sat down in front of my spiritual godparents, placed the *peitee* drum between my legs, sat up straight, and waited for their signal to beat the drum. They looked at me, and I looked at them. I smiled, and they did not smile. We waited. At this point, I had no idea of what I was to do or how I was to play.

I had seen enough drummers with all types of drums play exquisite rhythms. I had danced to some of the greatest drummers along the East Coast. I just knew that I understood drumming. We waited. They got up from their chairs and left without saying a word. I knew then that I was in trouble.

But something else was going on while we waited and waited, unbeknownst to me at the time. All the time we waited, I still had my knees and thighs wrapped around the drum. I had been unconsciously rubbing my hands lightly over the skin. Even when my behind started to hurt and my thighs started to cramp, I never let go.

As my confidence began to wane, I could feel the tears starting to rise. I am not a loser. I am a natural-born winner. Everyone has worked just as hard as I for my initiation into the priesthood, and now I don't know how to play the drum. All I could do then was to start rocking back and forth and back and forth, with the tears coming down my face as I sat alone in the compound circle with a couple of scrawny chickens and rib-showing dogs. They ignored me, and I ignored them.

There was a bird nearby singing, a dog barking from some other place. It was hot and dusty, and I was miserable. Where did everybody go? Where was I to go? I just kept rocking back and forth and back and forth, with tears pouring down my face.

All of a sudden, I felt a deep, heavy pressure start to rise up from the inside of my thighs. I wanted to panic, but I wouldn't let go. It was not a sensual pressure; it was beyond that. It continued to rise up my spine to my arms and then down to my hands. My hands raised high above my head. I slapped the drum so hard that I remember the pain clearly as if it were yesterday instead of fifty years ago.

My legs and thighs were glued to that drum; I couldn't let go if I wanted to. I raised my hands again and slapped down again much lighter. The sound was not flat, but it wasn't full either. I realized that I had stopped rocking, so I started up again but without the tears. I hit the drum with my right hand as I rocked forward. And when I rocked backward, I hit the drum with my left hand. Slow and steady, I hit the drum—first right hand, then left hand, rock forward with the right, and then rock backward with the left—keeping the rhythm steady. I began to feel the excitement rushing throughout my body into my hands. My fingers did start to ache, but I didn't stop. I felt the urge to hit once going forward and two hits going backward. The sound changed. Nobody came around me yet. At that point, I was hoping that no one did come. I knew I was still far away from playing any intricate rhythm. At times, I tried to work in an extra hit or two, but I lost my rhythm when I did. So I kept up the one forward and two backward.

I had no idea how long I was in that position beating the drum, but I didn't care. I knew that sooner or later, I was going to master that drum—perhaps not in a concert hall, but certainly in a ritual.

When the pain started to be stronger in my hands and thighs, I decided to release the drum and rest. My legs were hurting so intensely I knew that I would probably be bow-legged the rest of my life.

After waiting about another half an hour, my godparents returned. My lessons would start the next day, since the drum has now accepted me. I still couldn't move or pick up anything. My godmother bathed my hands with Florida water cologne and peppermint leaves to draw out the soreness. My hands started to swell and ache. My legs refused to unbend. I was a mess, and I looked it and felt it. I had to sit until my thighs agreed to release my knees and legs, and I hobbled to my cot to sleep for the rest of the day. I faintly remember hearing a lot of laughing in the background as I drifted off to sleep. I knew they were laughing at me, but I really didn't care very much. I'll do better tomorrow.

Tomorrow came, and I couldn't move a muscle; I was in agony. My hands were so swollen that I couldn't even bathe myself—my godmother had to do that; how humiliating.

After bathing me, my godmother gave me a strong bitter tea to drink. Even though it was sweetened, it still tasted awful.

Later that afternoon, I did begin to feel better, but there was to be no drum playing that day. It was three days before I approached that drum. I was now intimidated by that drum. I offered a strong silent prayer.

The lesson began. The pain was still coursing throughout my body, especially my wrists and hands. Rather than playing, I was taught technique, posture, arm position, feet position, and even head position. I was given the ins and the outs of producing the exact sound that I needed. Even though I was encouraged to play the drum, deep within me, I knew that the drum was not my true calling.

The drum would always be close to me, but it would not be my life's focus. However, I did learn to play well enough for my workshops, lectures, and rituals. Every time I get carried away with the spirit of the drum, my body aches for days. But a couple of Tylenol quickly takes care of that.

I know that the drum soothes me as well as inspires me. I teach that everyone can play the drum for their satisfaction and enjoyment by connecting heart to heart with the instrument. It does work.

Drumming

The Initiation of the Drum

*D*rums fascinate everyone, no matter the age or tradition. Every country, every religion, every tradition has their drum—a ceremonial drum that is sacred and has its own story. A strong legend has always followed the drum that makes it unique and exciting. The tourist trade brought about an insatiable appetite for buying drums for decoration and just plain acquisition, but they are just poor replicas of the great mother drum.

The drum is a divine entity with a voice that speaks to your heart and soul. It is the bridge between you and the invisible realms. If you hear the rhythms, your body will begin to move in such a fashion that you become totally immersed into its world. It can be exhilarating and frightening by releasing your pent-up anxieties, your deep fears, and even your pain, especially if you are alone with the drumming.

A sacred drum must be "baptized" by the medicine man upon its completion of being made. The entire village participates by bringing special sweets and foods for the enjoyment of everyone. Gifts and food must also be given to the drummers as well as the medicine man. Everyone knows the drum is capable of bringing messages from the ancestors, and now is not the time to be forgetful. This is a great occasion—a powerful event that occurs maybe twice a year, no more than that, and sometimes not at all.

All of the drums that have been made by the master drummer and/or his apprentices must lay in state for three days without being beaten. Usually, there is a special hut made just for the drums and this event. Each drum lays on the earth, and the gifts are laid around it, such as stones, shells, berries, or flowers. Every three hours, the food is exchanged for new food, from sunrise to sunset. The drums sleep at night. After the third day, the drums are brought to the center of the village by their owner. The final ritual is to begin.

The medicine man approaches the first drum with chants learned from long ago. Using a solution made from the boiling of leaves, twigs, and berries, he throws this "holy water" at the drum (making sure that none of it touches the skin heads). It may seem that he is yelling at the drum, even screaming, but the fact is that he is receiving the secret name of the drum, and no one else must hear it. Once the medicine man is satisfied that he has heard the proper name, he immediately whispers it to the drummer. That drummer smiles and salutes the medicine man with a short but very loud beating of his drum. The village screams and yells with approval. The medicine man raises his hand for silence and moves on to the next drummer.

After the last drum has been blessed, the medicine man begins to strut around the center of the village, and the drummers would raise their drums high above their heads and follow him. This is not a plain walking around in a circle by any means; there is a subtle rhythm coming out of the footsteps, their bodies begin to gently undulate, and the silent villagers sense the vibrations and begin to move their bodies ever so lightly with great anticipation of that which they know is to come. Babies are rushed to the outer circle to be minded by the younger girls. The men rush to form the outer circle around the parading drummers. The atmosphere is electrified with energy and passion; a fever-pitch high is felt by everyone. The time is very near for the great mother drum to speak for the very first time. The medicine man decides to toy with the drummers by making them wait until he finishes brandishing his wand of branches and leaves; his dance of blessing. Everyone is delighted. He signals the drummers to take their seats; he approaches the master drummer and bows deeply. The master drummer returns the salute. The village is still, even the babies are quiet. The master drummer knows that all eyes are upon him, but he is no longer aware of anyone or anything except that his beloved is resting between his knees; his hands are resting gently on her crown of taut skin, waiting for her signal to start. The perspiration starts to bead up on his forehead, his bare shoulders, his arms, the back of his hands. He waits. He is hardly breathing. He waits, he stares, and he can feel the blood rising up his legs to his thighs, straight through to his groin. He stiffens. The blood pumps harder as it reaches his heart, and then his hands raise up and come down on her skin with a sound that causes everyone to gasp. His hands raise again and come down, making a sound that causes him to shudder. He is connected—he is in her grasp, he is beating her rhythm, he is hearing her message—he is one with her. And the villagers cheer madly, and the medicine man signals the other drummers to join now.

Each drummer will remember their drum's secret name and rhythm. Each drummer is just as important as the master drummer but must wait to take his turn to salute and to be acknowledged. This drum blessing will take all night, but the dancing that ensues is so welcomed that everything is put away for this festive night.

In the days to come, new rhythms are made known to the drummers, and each rhythm is given a name recognized by that village, that tradition, that drummer, and the name should never change.

How to Make a Drum

The base of the drum is hollowed out from a sacred tree from the forest. But first, the drum maker must listen to the heartbeat of the tree. He must go from tree to tree to tree until he and only he can hear that beat. If he doesn't hear, then he doesn't cut. He will go back to the forest another day, she doesn't want him yet. He will hear that beat, ever so faintly, when she has chosen him. This is the time to be patient and trusting because now, he must approach with respect, admiration, and a need to love her. Only then will she allow him to continue the ritual. The ax must be sharp, and the blow must be sure, not raggedy or misshapen. Seven blows will bring her to his feet. He will rest with her between his legs and allow her to feel his heartbeat. Before he begins to hollow the drum of her insides, she must sit between his feet. He'll pull her close with his arms wrapped gently around her middle. He will rest his head on top of her head and be still like he's never been still before. The drum must smell him. She'll start with his feet. She'll know those feet have walked the earth of Africa. She will smell his groin and know that he is a true son of Africa. She will smell his hands and know that they have worked the soil of Africa. She'll feel his head and know that he has the passion for her. And then the final test—she will listen to his heartbeat and know that it can blend with hers. Then and only then may he begin to hollow her trunk, moving only to her rhythm and time. Nobody else can hear but him. He's got a long way to go before she's ready for him

He will feel the vibrations, the tension, and the release as he hollows out the drum because she has already determined her pitch, her sound, her depth. Her bark must be the last to go because now, she is naked—only for him. Her skin is pure but ragged and needs to be gently smoothed out all over. Now, the two of them rest. There is no hurry when one is creating a new soul.

She will choose the sacrificial animal for the fine skin to cover her crown of glory! He does not have to be the one to hunt the animal—it has already been done by the hunter.

The skin is thoroughly cleansed in the approved fashion of scraping both sides of the skin without tearing it. He keeps the skin cool; he keeps it moist so that he can stretch it continuously. He'll sing to it, hum to it, talk to it—direct the skin's focus to communicate for spirit. Scraping the skin is finished only when both sides are smooth and even—no hairs, no lumps or bumps, and best of all, no smell.

The prepared skin is now placed over the crown of the drum using pegs to help the real stretching. This part of the drum making takes a lot of time, patience, and spirit connection. So dig out the holes for the stretch pegs evenly around the crown. Start placing the skin over the holes and hammer in the pegs, pulling and coaxing but being ever so careful not to tear or rip the skin. Keep the skin cool and moist as you stretch her thin and even over the crown. After the last peg has been hammered into place, let her rest for one day and one night. You still have a long way to go before she becomes a drum.

The master drummer chuckles; she must sleep with you, eat with you, watch you, feel everything you feel before she makes the first sound. It takes much more than physical work to bring her into her spirit. You must speak to her in loving tones, sing to her of her value, and stroke her body, exclaiming her beauty. As you hold her between your knees, you will begin to feel her vibrations; that means her heart is beginning to mix with your heart. Take it slow now or she'll get away from you.

Remember, the medicine man must bless her with the proper herbs and water before her first sound, her first rhythm, her first breath. Dedicate her to the deities and the ancestors to bring forth the communications. Pronounce her to the forest from where she came as the mother of all drums. She is the symbol of the moon and the sun and the heartbeat of the universe. She is older than mankind because she carries the memory of the beginning in every fiber of her being. She waited just for you to be ready for her.

Each time you embrace her, a symbol will start to come alive in your heart that she wants you to carve on her body, usually one at a time. This is not decoration; this is supernatural power between the two of you. Now stand her away from you. Sit down and watch her with no distractions. Watch her as she begins to taunt you. Feel her as she begins to lure you. Listen to her as she begins to send her sound into your heart, your thighs, your head, and then into your hands. Then and only then can you strike her thin beautiful skin. Never forget that first sound because you will never hear it again from any drum that you make. That sound which comes from the depths of her heart will live within you forever. She is now ready to join with you in sound and beauty. She is ready to bring her message to all who will listen. She is ready to force the rhythm from your heart to answer her. No one will be able to refuse her; she is ready to jump with joy. She'll part with her rhythms for every occasion, and she'll name each one. And each cadence will be etched in your soul. Now, beat the drum.

The master drummer reminds the drum maker to feed her once a week with yams, millet, and berries. Place the food in front of her. After three hours, you eat all of the food in her special plate because she ate the spiritual essence and you eat the physical essence. Let her rest now because tomorrow you will introduce her to the village, the forest, the animals, the mountains, the heavens, all who will hear her. As you sleep tonight, she will enter your dreams with her rhythms as words, her beat as her true feelings, her vibrations of her love for you. Sleep now because tomorrow, when you strike out her sound, you will know absolute joy.

The master drummer gives his final thoughts: remember, the drum is the first instrument of the world made exclusively for the communication between you and spirit. You talk to her, and she will speak her passwords to you only. You must build the trust and loyalty with her in order to gain her true sounds. Her sounds come from the deepest cavities of the earth, and they will rise to the farthest star. The both of you are needed to make this happen. Carve your wants, desires, and hopes on her trunk. Let your sweat quench her thirst, and let the calluses on your hands be the key that opens her secret chamber. She knows you now, she smells you now. She feels your heat, your rhythm, your desire. You are as one now. May you keep the rhythm as pure as you receive it.

Even though there are all kinds of drums available throughout the world, there is one constant theme: they are all round. Regardless of the size, the drum must be round.

Our ecological system calls for other materials to be used to make drums. Our trees are suffering, and our animals, whose skin once fitted over the drum, are becoming extinct. So the old ways are being replaced. The master drummer has a dilemma: what is he to do now?

This initiation must always be presented as a gift. Never is it to be sold or bartered. And in return, a generous gift may be given to the donor. There will be times when the drum will sound flat and even feel lifeless. One must listen to the master drummer who will tell you how and when the skin needs to be tightened. There are many Western drummers who tighten the skin by holding it over an open fire or even passing the flame of a candle over the head. The type of skin used today will determine the quality of the drum. Pig skin, goat skin, and cow skin are used for the tourist trade which now cannot be brought into the United States because of the diseased animals.

When you cannot make the sound come from the drum and the skin is tight and everything else seems to be in order, then sit alone with the drum and just look at her for as long as you can. Don't try to play her yet; being familiar with the energy of the drum is the primary goal before playing. Your rhythm must blend with her rhythm. Most people have lost their soul rhythm, but it can be found—be patient. It's like trying to find your swing; it's not like anyone else's swing or sound or rhythm. Don't try to be fancy, just be slow and steady. You will connect with the rhythm of the drum, no matter what kind it is.

The drum is the heartbeat of the soul. It is the rhythm of the universe. It is the messenger of the gods. Treat it as such. Now you can beat it until both of your hearts are content.

Final Thoughts

A rose by any other name is still a rose.

Hence, religions from all over the world have had their foundations formed by traditions and beliefs stemming from indigenous peoples. Shamanism is the foundation of religion as it is today.

So many of the Shaman's spiritual practices have been adopted and adapted by the organized religions of the world. The pomp and circumstance that accompanies ceremony are derived from the tribal rituals of ancient times. Even the dates have been kept intact. These same "holy" days have new or different names to identify the religion, but the fact remains that the shamanistic "holy" days, such as the Day of the Dead (Halloween) and Winter Solstice (Christmas), as well as the many annual feast days, are celebrated throughout the world on a daily basis.

Fortunately, everyone is quite aware, if not knowledgeable, of the various traditions and religions that are still in practice today. Understanding these beliefs is not the focus; however, acknowledgment and respect by everyone is the goal. Judgment must not be the task of anyone concerning the validity of any belief, tradition, or religion.

During my research, I recognized the unbreakable thread common among indigenous peoples of the world. That everlasting thread is the firm belief in the natural elements as well as all living creatures.

Mountains, rivers, trees, boulders, as well as all animals and birds all represent some form of god, goddess, and/or spirit. These supernatural beings protect guide, teach, heal, and fertilize the land as well as the man and woman. Specific days were set aside for worship. Gifts would be prepared according to the characteristics of the deity. Various costumes made of feathers, leaves, shells, vines, colored clay, or animal remnants would be worn. Only when other religions conquered or persuaded these peoples did the beliefs slowly begin to change and shift their focus on other beliefs. Many people changed over because might is right or even because of the idea that the grass is greener on the other side. However, many held fast to their beliefs and are still practicing the original rituals as far as the law will allow—"Might is right!"

Religion will always have an important role in our daily lives. It influences our politics through the legitimate religious-based organizations that influence segments of government; our economics by way of dictating the ceremonial aspect of marriage, birth, and death; and our psychological status by dictating acceptable standards of fair play and morals. Actually, there is no part of our daily lives that has not been touched by some religious input, regardless of faith and creed.

Wherever you go, religion is at hand in some fashion or some form; therefore, it behooves everyone to show respect and acknowledgment to all beliefs regardless of how primitive it may appear. It does seem that the pantheon of gods, goddesses, ancestors, and entities are on the comeback trail, and they're not too happy.

African initiations are a prime example of the beliefs of one people that are misunderstood by another people who seem bent on condemning and destroying any belief that is different.

Initiations are a sacred bond between man, community, and creator/God; it is a deeply rooted act of allegiance to the ancestor and to all the spirits of the heavens and of the lands. Initiation serves as a foundation for mankind to build and sustain the character of his being. Initiation connects the soul.

Suggested Exercises

All rituals have a basic foundation consisting of the following:

- Intention of ritual
- Candles, incense, flowers, and water or wine
- A small surface to serve as an altar
- Prayers (what it is you want to achieve)
- Short hymn, mantra, or chant (optional)

Any celebration can be as simple or as elaborate as desired. Time, money, and patience are the key factors in designing any ritual. Participation can be for one or up to hundreds. The goal is to acknowledge an important event in life.

Listed below are examples of intentions. Intention means the purpose for your ritual.

>My intention for this ritual is to celebrate the birth of (name of child).

>My intention for this ritual is to acknowledge the passage of (name) into adulthood.

Giving the reason for your ritual defines a definite course of energy and direction for all of the participants. Intention sets the mood and pace; the spiritual stage is now ready for the action.

Even though announcements and invitations have stated the nature of the event, it is best to restate the intention at the beginning of the ritual. Once this has been completed, the second part of the ritual begins.

Preparing the altar

A table or some adequate space on which to place a candle (usually white), a glass of water (a beautiful goblet or fancy glass), two or three incense sticks in a holder (sandalwood, or Blue Nile, or any sweet smelling incense. Some prefer charcoals and then placing bulk incense on the hot coals. Use anything that pleases you), lastly, a bowl of fruit and/or fine breads. Symbolically, the candle represents fire and is set in the southern direction. The water represents itself and is set in the western direction. The incense represents air and is set in the eastern direction. The fruit, bread, or flowers is set in the northern direction and represents the earth.

North

Flowers, bread, etc.

West	East
Water	Incense

South

Fire—candle

Light the incense and the candles. Use a lighter or something other than a match because the odor of sulfur from the match is unpleasant. Face the altar, standing to face the eastern direction, if possible.

Start now with a prayer from your tradition, such as the Lord's Prayer or the Twenty-third Psalm or Hail Mary. Usually, everyone knows them and can recite with you. However, you may write your own prayer or use a prayer from your religious tradition.

The prayer explains what it is you want to manifest, and you are addressing your petition to God or Buddha or Krishna or any sacred source. This prayer is a plea from your heart to the heart of your belief.

Examples of prayers that could be used for any occasion:

Prayers of Intention

I

Oh Blessed One, we who are gathered here for this sacred
    event beseech Thee for Thy Blessings
Hear our petitions and grant us our heart's desire.
Send forth Thy mercy and love,
For we are in need of Your miraculous love and compassion.
Hear, Oh Sacred One,
our cries of woe and our pleas for Your blessed intervention.
Bless us. Heal us. Love us.
For which we shall always give thanks.
Amen.

II

May Your light shine upon us
and Your countenance be forever in our hearts.
We come before Thee with bowed head and bended knee to
    receive Thy Holy Blessings.
Allow Your Divine Grace to forever shroud us in Your perpetual
    Glory.
Be merciful unto us who adore Thee.
Be forgiving unto us who acknowledge Thy Divineness.
Our hearts remain open to receive Thy guidance.
Our minds remain alert to hear Your call.
Our voices sing aloud Your praises.
Be forever mindful of the wonder of Your creation in whom
    You have placed Your Divine Love.
And for this we do give thanks.
Amen.

III

Oh Divine One,
As I walk this great Earth, speak to me through Your trees, Your flowers, Your fowl, Your fishes and every living creature;
That I may be aware of my bountiful blessings and Your abundant love.
May I ever be so humble to be generous in sharing Your compassion and patience.
May Your Divine Light shine through me and all around me to touch all who come into my presence.
Allow me to learn and to know all the wondrous miracles of Your creation.
Know that my heart is filled with gladness to praise Your Divine Existence.
Walk with me forever and forever.
Amen.

IV

Dinner Blessing

We are blessed with air that allows us to breathe.
We are blessed with water that bathes away our waste as well as quenches our thirst.
We are blessed with the good earth that grows our food and allows us to live on her.
We are blessed with Fire that gives us warmth and cooks our food.
We are forever thankful for the many blessings that we receive every day of our lives. Amen. Amen. Amen.

V

Prayer to the Ancestors

I am the future of my powerful ancestors; I am the hope for all human kind.
I am in perfect harmony with all that lives and breathes. I am aware that as I grow, so do my responsibilities as a young man (or woman) grow.

Therefore, I will speak with kindness to everyone;
I will act with thoughtfulness with everyone;
And when I receive, no matter what it is, I shall do so with great humility.
I am the breath of God!
I am the wisdom of the Goddess!
I am the son (or daughter) of the universe!
I am truly a blessed and privileged young man (woman).
For which I give thanks, I give thanks, I give thanks!
Amen. Amen. Amen.

VI

Prayer to Papa

Papa wherever you are, I am with you.
I can feel you.
I can hear you.
I can see you.
I pray for your success, your good health, and your happiness.
I pray to be in your heart, your thoughts, and your memories, as you are always in mine.
I love you papa.
Amen. Amen. Amen.

Once the prayers have been completed, it is suggested that some form of music, chant, or mantra follows. Perhaps someone could sing or play an instrument or play some recorded music.

Some of the well-known chants are listed below. A chant means repeating one word or one sentence over and over again; a mantra means singing that word or one sentence over and over again, on one note or rhythmical chord.

Chants and Mantras

I
Adigaba, makoumbey
II
Onah, dumah, teemah

III
Asham. Asham nay dole.

(This energy will start to build into a spiral for healing.)

Repeat at least five minutes without stopping. This section can last as long as you want. It is an uplifting and energizing experience that blends a group together completely for the intended purpose of the ritual. And it is enjoyable.

Now is the time for the presentation—the main course, as it were.

Body of the Ritual

Exercise 1

In the Western world, many traditions practice some form of "scarification" or symbols for "identifying" your family traditions. Piercing the ears of an infant in order to wear gold earrings; boys wear gold chains. Some parents give gold bands to infants for protection, blessings, successful life, as well as for beauty.

Invite maternal and paternal grandparents (if possible) to an afternoon ritual for a *"bonding with the ancestors" celebration.*

Sometimes there can be three, four, and five generations to participate in this beautiful ceremony.

Before everyone arrives, place a small table in the center of the room; cover it with a white cloth or towel. Place the following items on the table:

- Small amount of uncooked white rice
- Small amount of honey/small silver spoon
- Small amount of milk
- Three long-stemmed flowers of any kind

Family and friends should gather around the table. The parents then bring the child up to the table and state their intentions, such as the following:

> We give thanks for this miracle in our lives.
> We give thanks to the ancestors who made this possible.

> We honor all of our family ancestors in dedicating our child to
> the divine will of our sacred bloodline

The infant is then passed to the maternal grandparents for a prayer. The grandmother should pour the grains of rice over the head of the reclining baby while saying a short prayer for the baby, which should include the purpose of the rice over the head. Rice represents the earth's abundance and prosperity that is the child's claim.

The grandfather then places a small amount of honey to the baby's mouth while saying a prayer for the future of the child. Honey represents the sweet nature of life that is the child's claim. The next grandmother then pours the milk over the baby's head while saying a short prayer. Milk represents the life-sustaining force of Mother Earth that is the child's claim.

The final grandparent then holds the child and passes the flowers back and forth over the child while saying a prayer. The flowers represent the beauty of the earth that is the child's claim.

Finally, each person present should speak their prayer for the child.

The parents should thank everyone and then complete the ceremony with a festive lunch. Bringing gifts for the baby is not necessary, but it is the decision of the parents.

Before, During, and After Delivery of a Baby

Exercise 2—Welcoming

Once a pregnancy has been determined and announced, it should be decided to have a "welcoming ritual" with family and friends as soon as possible.

Tools needed:

- A small table to act as an altar
- A tablecloth for the table/altar
- Cloth strips of red, green, yellow, and sky blue

> Place the yellow strip on the edge of the table representing east
> (where the sun rises).

Place the red strip of cloth on the edge of the table representing south.

Place the sky blue strip of cloth on the edge of the table representing west (where the sun sets).

Place the green strip of cloth on the edge of the table representing the north.

- Two white candles (paraffin or bee's wax)
- A glass wine goblet or a pretty glass (no plastic)
- Small metal dish to burn incense or use an incense holder
- Two fresh flowers of whatever color you prefer
- A small loaf of bread or a bread roll or even stone-wheat crackers
- ½ cup of white rice (preferably unbleached)

If there are pictures of grandparents, place them on the altar opposite each other. If not, perhaps something that was precious to the family.

Performing the exercise:

- Light the candle and incense
- Gather family and friends in a full or semicircle around the altar. The mother-to-be and the father stand in front of the altar.
- Begin by welcoming everyone for attending at this special time.

Both mother and father should read aloud together the following invocation:

Divine Creator/God/Goddess, Buddha, Krishna (or whatever your choice may be). We who are gathered in this sacred circle desire to be blessed with your light and love. Our intent is to welcome the new life that has been gifted to us and our families and ancestors. We give thanks to honor you by bringing forth this new soul yet ancient spirit. We now extend our vows to include the welfare and safety of our child. With unconditional love we shall guide him in the ways of truth, courage, honesty, love, and understanding. He will have respect for parents, family, and ancestors. We shall teach our child to be respectful to everyone and everything, albeit animals, birds, everything of the earth, and most importantly, respect for self. We beseech thee to grant us the wisdom and patience and strength to guide this child through life as a caring, giving, and wondrous human being.

For this we give thanks. Amen!

The entire gathering can sing a song of devotion, a chant, or mantra. Have the words printed for the group to sing together.
Declarations for the Infant:

The parents should begin the most important aspect of the ceremony by verbalizing their desires, directions, and goals they want for their child. When both parents have finished their declaration, they then turn to face the group. Starting to the parents' right, the first person in the semicircle then walks to the center of the circle facing the parents. This person will read or speak aloud their commitments to this child. When finished, he/she then returns to the circle, and the next person comes forward to do the same thing. When everyone has completed their declaration, they all join hands to form a complete circle.

Chant the following mantra for five minutes or longer if you desire:

We are the circle of protection, light, and love!

Everyone then drops their hands and faces the altar. The expectant mother then approaches the altar and picks up the incense. Raising it above her head, she then speaks out loud the following phrase:

May the East grant our child knowledge and wisdom.

She then returns the incense. The expectant father then approaches the altar and picks up the goblet or glass of water. Raising it above his head, he then speaks out loud the following phrase:

> May the West grant our child sensitivity, creativity, and compassion.

He then returns the goblet to the altar. The mother then raises the bread above her head and says the following phrase:

> May the North grant our child abundance and prosperity.

She then returns the bread to the altar. The father then picks up the candle and raises it above his head and speaks the following:

> May the South grant our child the determination and courage to be of service to humankind.

He then returns the candle to the altar. The expectant parents then face each other and embrace and then face the semicircle. Each person comes forward to embrace the mother-to-be and congratulate the father. Meanwhile, a favorite song or chant is to be sung until all have made their greetings. The ceremony ends with everyone saying the following:

> And it is done.
> So mote it be.
> Amen, amen, amen

Now is the time to serve the food and drink.

When everyone has finished eating, the soon-to-be parents should sit together to open the gifts for the baby.

This ends the ceremony.

Exercise 3—Labor and Delivery

This ritual gathering should be the choice of the mother as to who should be with her during her labor and delivery. If she does want a few family members and friends to be in attendance, then they should know beforehand what is expected from them in order to support her and the baby.

If at this time she decides it is too nerve-wracking to have so many people around her, then that group should move to another place. In the event she wants the company around her, here are a few suggestions to support her at this time:

- Hum a song she likes softly
- Recite a poem, a Bible verse, or prayer that she likes

The group can also do a breathing exercise such as this: inhale for three counts; hold that breath for three counts; release the breath in three counts; and hold that emptiness for three counts. Repeat from inhale. Do this round at least seven times. I recommend closing the eyes while doing this breathing exercise. Also, when you exhale, vocalize the sound of "hah."

Concentrate on finding the core of her pain, and then send white light from your heart center to that pain center. This will allow the pain to quickly do its work and, believe it or not, ease the mother with any discomfort. It does work!

Once the baby is born, everyone present should say "We give thanks" three times. Then allow the parents to rest and be with their newborn child.

With my daughter, we planned all of the activities she wanted during labor and delivery ahead of time. Afterwards, we served hot tea and finger sandwiches because of the late hour.

We ran a lukewarm bath for my daughter and my new grandson to bond and relax and at the same time to give thanks. All I could think of at that moment, as I sat beside the tub, was that there had to be a God somewhere; what a wondrous event. Of course, everyone started to cry, even the midwives, and especially the proud and grateful father. I could hardly wait for the next time, but I knew that she didn't want to hear such "nonsense." I kept my thoughts to myself; there was too much joy to celebrate. Nevertheless, two and a half years later, we were blessed with my granddaughter, and it was even better the second time around.

Exercise 4—The Ritual for Christening, Baptism, or Presenting the Newborn

Whatever title you use isn't the issue. The intent is the focus of this ritual. All traditions and denominations can use this ritual without being offended.

Because hospitals have finally become patient friendly, it is now acceptable to request our baby's placenta (afterbirth), or at least part of it. There are special containers available to hold the placenta until needed for ritual. However, it should be frozen to hold off decomposition.

This ritual can be performed by one person or a large group.

A sapling should be selected for its heartiness in your climate because it will represent the spirit of the newborn—as the child grows, so does the tree.

Assuming you have space for the planting of a tree, a deep hole should be dug about one day ahead of the scheduled ritual. (My tradition begins the ritual at noon, and a lunch is served afterwards.) However, select a time that is comfortable for you and your guests.

All invited guests and family members should bring a small gift for the tree planting, such as a quartz crystal, a decorated egg (raw), a semiprecious stone, or anything that represents the earth element. Some present a song or a poem.

Everyone forms a circle around the opening (hole) with their gifts. The officiate should announce the reason and/or intent of this special event. Lead the group into a song, a mantra, or a prayer. Meanwhile, the parent or parents should be seated within the circle facing each other as the mother holds the child. The father should sit on the east side of the hole, while the mother and child should sit on the west.

The officiate then invokes from the east, the west, the north, and finally, the south. He then retreats. The parents should both stand and raise the infant above their heads. The father then speaks first:

> Thanks for the birth of the infant.
> Thanks to the ancestors for giving them a lifeline to carry on.
> The father then speaks of his wants, desires, hopes, and commitments to and for this child.
> The mother also speaks of thanks, ancestors, desires, etc. They then both sit down; this time, they should sit side by side symbolizing the shared responsibilities and dreams for their child.

The father then empties the placenta into the hole for the tree. The officiate then returns to lead the group in a song or chant. If the group has rattles, drums, or any reasonable instrument, this would be the perfect time to include them in the ritual.

The officiate then signals the group to end the song. The gift giving, one person at a time, begins with the officiate being the first to speak of his gift and the reasons for his choice. The gift is placed in the hole (on top of the placenta). When all gifts have been placed in the hole, the father plants the tree. The final act is for the officiate and the parents to walk the circle, handing the infant to each person for each to gently whisper a prayer, a word, a hope, a dream, or a desire into the baby's ear; after which, the baby is handed back to the officiate. They should move to the next person, and so on, until the entire group has each held the baby.

Returning to the center of the circle, the parents then anoint the child. First, the mother, with water dripped gently over the forehead; after which, the father places a tiny drop of oil on the forehead of the baby. They both raise the baby over their heads and say the following words together with the group:

> It is done!
> So mote it be.
> Amen, amen, amen.

The parents and child depart with the officiate, and the group follows with song and merriment. The feast begins, and the ceremony is completed.

Supplemental Reading

Flash of the Spirit, Robert Farris Thompson, Paperback, August 1984, Random House; ISBN: 0394723694

Sacred Possessions: *Voodoo, Santeria, Obeah, and the Caribbean*, Margarite Fernandez Olmos, Lizabeth Paravisini-Gebert, Eds., Paperback March 1997, Rutgers Univ Press; ISBN: 0813523613

Tell My Horse: Voodoo and Life in Haiti and Jamaica, Zora Neale Hurston, Reissue edition (February 1990), HarperCollins (paper); ISBN: 0060916494

Mules and Men, Zora Neale Hurston, Reissue edition (March 1990), HarperCollins (paper); ISBN: 0060916486

The Healing Wisdom of Africa: *Finding Life Purpose Through Nature, Ritual, and Community*, Malidoma Patrice Somé, L. M. Somé, Paperback (October 1999), J P Tarcher; ISBN: 087477991X

Of Water and the Spirit: Ritual, Magic, and Initiation in the Life of an African Shaman, Malidoma Patrice Somé, Reprint edition (May 1995), Penguin USA (Paper); ISBN: 0140194967

Welcoming Spirit Home: Ancient African Teachings to Celebrate Children and Community, Sobonfu E. Somé (September 1999), New World Library; ISBN: 1577310098

The Spirit of Intimacy: Ancient Afrian Teachings in the Ways of Relationships, Sobonfu E. Somé, 1st Quill edition (January 2000), Quill; ISBN: 0688175791

African Holistic Health: Complete Herb Remedy Guide, Disease Treatment, Nutrition, Diet, Wholistic Perspectives, African Herb History, Self Diagnosis, Llaila O. Afrika, (October 1993), A & B Book Pub Dist; ISBN: 1881316718

African Spirituality: On Becoming Ancestors, Anthony Ephirim-Donkor, (March 1997), Africa World Press Inc.; ISBN: 0865435537

www.ingramcontent.com/pod-product-compliance
Lightning Source LLC
Chambersburg PA
CBHW032126090426
42743CB00007B/478